SPEED AND POLITICS

SEMIOTEXT(E) FOREIGN AGENTS SERIES

Oiginally published in 1977 as "Vitesse et Politique," Édition Galilée, Paris.

Published by Semiotext(e)
2007 Wilshire Blvd., Suite 427, Los Angeles, CA 90057
www.semiotexte.com

Special thanks to Nicholas Zurko and Mark Polizzotti.

Cover: Map of Paris published in 1847 depicting Baron Georges Eugène Haussman's plan to transform Paris into "the capital of capitals." In red are the networks of new streets and boulevards and in green are the parks. Courtesy of the New York City Public Library.
Back Cover Photography: Sylvère Lotringer
Design: Hedi El Kholti

ISBN-10: 1-58435-040-7
ISBN-13: 978-1-58435-040-8
Distributed by The MIT Press, Cambridge, Mass. and London, England
Printed in the United States of America

SPEED AND POLITICS

Paul Virilio

Translated by Marc Polizzotti

<e>

Contents

Benjamin H. Bratton

Logistics of Habitable Circulation

A brief introduction to the 2006 edition of *Speed and Politics*

> *If there had never been a war, I would have made a very good architect.*
>
> — Ahmed Shah Masoud, Afghan opposition leader reportedly assassinated 9.9.01 by suicide bombers who were, it is assumed, trained by Osama Bin-Ladan on behalf of the Taliban, as quoted in the *Los Angeles Times*, the morning edition of September 11, 2001.

PAUL VIRILIO'S MODERNITY is *logistical.* It doesn't directly deal with war, but with everything that makes it possible. Logistics is the preparation for war through the transfer of the nation's potential to its armed forces in time of peace as in times of war.[1] Modernity is a world in motion, expressed in translations of strategic space into logistical time, and back again. It is a history of cities, partitions, trading circuits, satellites, and software; of a political landscape governed by competing technologies of surveillance, mobilization, fortification and their interdependent administrations. It begins as an archaelogy of naval routes, strategic techniques and urban distributions, and becomes an integrated world of events reduced to shapes and symbols, viewed and manipulated instantaneously on screens. In Virilio's narrative, architectural regimes become computational, and vice versa. Both are logistical media for mobilization and its administration, technologies that consolidate territory into logistical fields and enable a Modern governance based on the abstracted calculation over omnidirectional spaces and surfaces, from open oceans to shared spreadsheets. This comprehensive technologization of the globe signals for Virilio both integration and disintegration, both control and accident. And it is finally through the accident, the realization of the imminent, irreducible risk that logistics hopes to contain, and not through control, that the strongest bonds of the *polis* are formed. For Virilio, they are an exceptional condition already contained within, and rigorously predicated by the invention that made them possible.

In the 1960's, Virilio collaborated with architect Claude Parent to develop a challenging program for an oblique architecture using inclined planes. It followed the principle of "habitable circulation," intending to radically expand the usable surface of urban landscape. His work as a theorist from the mid-1970's to today can be seen as a retroactive thesis on the possibility of such an architecture, and an ultimate abandonment of it in the face of other emerging spatial media. "The focus of my research," Virilio noted, "has shifted from topology to dromology, i.e., the study and analysis of the increasing speed of transport and communications on the development of land-use."[2] The image of the 'polis' (city) as a dynamic, vehicular landscape is both Virilio's initial architectural solution and his eventual theoretical warning. "Dromology" (from Gr. *dromos*: race course) is this government of differential motility, of harnessing and mobilizing, incarcerating and accelerating things and people. His third book, *Vitesse et Politique / Speed and Politics* (1977, 1986, 2006) is a history of what he calls an "inevitable technological vitalism" through which multiple projectiles—the inert membranes of fortress and bunkers, the "metabolic bodies" of soldiers, and transport bodies of naval vessels—mutually prostheticize each other in a pursuit of the competitive advantage of speed.[3] Among the key metabolic transformations traced in the book is the movement from the urban fortress to the open, smooth glacis of the sea, now a "vast logistical camp" in which naval, and finally amphibious strategies organize a "right to the sea." This in turn framed a "right to the road" and later diagrammed the land in the smooth image of maritime drift. In that shift, the condition of habitable circulation, and its origins in military logistics—mobilization and fortification—remains of critical importance. What was once asked of architecture, though, is now accomplished by other means, both informational and computational. Now the presence and vehicular movement of people and objects through global space is tightly integrated with an infrastructure of software, and to send objects in motion or to impede their trajectory is a logistical labor performed by pulses of light as much as flesh and steel.

"…An Essay on Dromology"

Speed and Politics was first published in Paris against a backdrop characterized by the complicit, symmetrical stand-off of nuclear superpowers sealed by the SALT II accords, as well as by the rise of political terrorism in London, Rome, Mogadishu, Stammheim, Phnom Penh, Palestine, etc. By then, May 1968 (to which Virilio owed his appointment as Director of the École Spéciale d'Architecture) had soured into a restless, if also fertile, malaise. A new French society was reconfiguring itself around audiovisual media:

the kitsch utopia of *Beaubourg*, the commercial center buried underneath the *Forum des Halles*, the new information headquarters at *La Défense*, followed by the nightly spectacles at *Bercy*. Perhaps this had to be expected. Didn't *Mai* end with a dour Pres. de Gaulle going on television, instead of appearing in person on the balcony of the Hôtel de Ville, as would have been the custom? The anti-climactic broadcasts managed to accomplish through the single-channel television something no urban strategy could have done: to stop the tumult of the deterritorialized streets, and to bring the nation if not to order, then to attention, to fix their gazes on a new national center, not of buildings, but of *screens*.

Virilo's work from this period can be understood as a sort of immediate pre-history of the "Software Society."[4] By 1986, and the time of this English translation, the problematics of information technology, computational technologies (particularly database and optical media) had displaced the city (it reappeared in his later work, but as a artifact of the media that had partially consumed its earlier functions).

Virilio's logistical Modernity is meant "to carve and guide the masses," the metabolic multitude, into mobile trajectories. Dromology is a shifting, restless logistics of differential governance transforming the raw material of the world and rendering it "in a more appropriate form" (36). For Virilio, "The city is but a stopover, a point on a the synoptic path of a trajectory, the ancient military glacis, ridge road, frontier or riverbank, where the spectator's glance and the vehicle's speed of displacement were instrumentally linked. As I have said in the past, there is only habitable circulation" (31). Cities govern these multiple scales of relative object velocity. They accelerate and /or frustrate: "All [cities] are uncertain places because they are situated between two speeds of transit, acting as brakes against the acceleration of penetration" (33). As a technology of space, cities galvanize both human and non-human metabolisms, channeling them, amplifying them, concentrating them into centers, domesticating them into suburbs. The question that would animate much of Virilio's subsequent work is: how have these core functions of the city been assumed by other dromological media?

Our Logistical Modernities

"History progresses at the speed of its weapons systems;" that is, at the speed of the competitive capacities to envision, draw, map, curtail, mobilize, contour, stabilize and police the polis (90). At least since Vitruvius defined the rules of architecture based on his own military engineering experience, it is understood that the design of space is already a strategic weapon of fortification. But architectural media are only one such means and the evolution of their deployments is interrelated and serpentine. Marquis de Vauban, Louis XIV's chief military engineer of fortifications (and of their breaching), made to his king the unusual recommendation that in order to secure a less permeable border with France's neighbors he should voluntarily cede contested land deemed "indefensible." The plan realized Richelieu's earlier image to France as "le pré carré,"or the "squared field," and in fact this same phrase was later used to describe Vauban's parallel lines of fortifications up and down the now consolidated national enclosure. In 1782, Charles de Fourcroy's *tableau poliometrique* appeared. This "first known flowchart" is a diagram of the relative sizes of European metropoles, and in it, as geographer Gilles Palsky notes, "We see the passage to abstract, to fictitious features. By these proportional triangles, [de Fourcroy] constructs an image that does not return or relate to [the] original existence."[5] De Fourcroy's semiotic innovation was this figural territorialization, the drawing of the comparative scale of cities as relative, primary geometric forms. This "map" does not correspond to any direct representation of the geographic juxtaposition of the cities, but rather graphs their relative quantitative difference in the population. This inscription produces another *virtual* space with which to order the natural territory of the polis as a projected image of an enclosed, administrative totality.

For Virilio, this also signals the production of logistical space as a Modern administrative horizon. "This means the universe is redistributed by the military engineers, the earth 'communicating' like a single glacis, as the infrastructure of future battlefield," not one limited by given terrestrial geography (85). With the French Army of Engineers being assigned the task in 1790 of "expand[ing] the logistical glacis over the whole territory," this era marked the birth of Modern administration-by-calculation, an on-going project in which all of the vicissitudes of land and its inhabitants are continuously charted, symbolized, and manipulated. Virilio locates its emergence in the history of military geography, especially naval techniques. "Total war is omnipresent; it is first waged on the sea because the naval glacis naturally presents no permanent obstacle to vehicular movement of planetary dimensions," and the mobility of smooth maritime space would return to organize land in its logistical image (73). Governance by speed (by states or otherwise) is *logistics*, and logistics, like the oceanic vectors from which it is born, is omnidirectional.

Today the speed of logistics is also largely computational, but this is not to say virtual, immaterial, or distant. Quite the contrary. Supermarket shelves, for example, are a human interface to a vast *internet of things*: a network of supply-chain, demand-chain and customer-relationship management softwares, steel containers, offshore factories, inter-modal exchange protocols—all forming an unimaginably complex, robust and nimble assembly of everyday purchase commands with vast economies of production and distribution. Today's "fleets-in-being" are the exabytes and gigatons of component inventories in permanent transit, hurtling between trade zones as the consumable artifacts of their sponsoring corporations' technological and legal efficiencies. Finally, these (disin)corporations and their far-flung suppliers of parts, labor, and expertise, guard nothing so dearly as the legal agency of *brands*, those operational fictions which they so carefully embed into the demographically-microsegmented experiential touch-points of everyday life. This "flat world" imagines itself as slippery, oceanic grid modulated by differentially transporting, activating, internalizing, and/or prophylactically exteriorizing technologies: from shipping ports to aerotropoli, from banking software GUIs (graphical user interfaces) to web browser layout engines and data security protocols. Like an Andreas Gursky photograph, this "frictionless" landscape of interconnected objects and subjects is the constitution of a new architecture, one that relies on fragile alibis of virtual immateriality and procedural transparency to achieve the political, economic efficacy it enjoys. The reality of its performance, however, is also a uncontrollable accumulation of—very real and opaque—unintended consequences.

Dromocracy: Government by Prosthetics

Where does Virilio locate the historical agency of dromology (speed) and *dromocracy* (politics)? How does one become the other? The recurring actor in Virilio's history is the *State*, if only because it is also the legal signatory of modern war. But his is hardly a traditional political theory. "In fact there is no 'industrial revolution' but only a 'dromocratic revolution;' there is not democracy, only dromocracy; there is not strategy, only dromology" (69). States employ dromological techniques to exercise power, but as for Foucault, state apparatuses are functions, artifacts even, of dromocratic machinations that exceed their constitutions and incorporations. For Virilio (in concert with Deleuze and Guattari) such state governments are profiled as a sort of "machinic species" of collective formation. Echoing Heidegger, he writes that "dromocratic intelligence is not exercised against a more or less determined military adversary, but as a permanent assault on the world, and through it, on human nature" (86). Likewise, the mobilization of economic production is characterized less in terms of maximizing surplus labor value than according to the distribution of metabolic intensification in the service of an historically comprehensive acceleration.

Dromocracy establishes and reproduces standardized forms of assembly and disassembly for the systematic integration of human energy into specific infrastructures. "Factory work must not escape the dictatorship of movement. It reproduces the enclosure on the spot, in the obligatory and absurd kinetic cycle... a condensed machine of the logistical glacis" (101). This is the design of corporeal discipline in the pursuit of the image of speed [not the image of truth as Foucault might prioritize it] in which "the class struggle is replaced by the struggle of the technological bodies of the armies according to their dynamic efficiency: *logistics*" (72). Indeed the exercise of political authority in and through the dimensions of the body-in-motion appears for Virilio in its most extreme and comic form in those performances of collective singularization that are Marxist state stadium pageants. Their choreographies of motor functions move according to the party line, now a literal grid. The numb aesthetic of "miming the joys at being liberated" and through this, "the simplicity of a power that comes down to the constraint and housebreaking of bodies," is repeated upside down in the camps where the misbeliever's body absorbs the cultivation of the law (55). Virilio writes, "His dissidence is a *postural* crime" (56). Even today, as this script of fleshly discipline has largely been exported from the commanding G8 metropoles to its satellites, another softer intercourse emerges between the individual and his logistical destiny, transposed into other symbolic and informational economies.

Dromocracy depends on technologies that in their employment, straddle the pre-political and the hyperpolitical, working on the bodies of the masses as a practical material that can be strategically designed and deployed. If the city is a collective prostheses of its inhabitants, other technologies are for a more *individual*, specific purpose, for example the *car*. "The transportation capacity created by the mass production of automobiles became a social assault on space" that would undo centripetal urban concentration exploding it into the congested network of the open highway (50). "No more riots, no need for much repression; to empty the streets, it's enough to promise everyone the highway: this is the aim of [the Nazi party's] Volkswagen plebiscite" (49). Dromocracy extends to this new platform: "Speed limits...we are talking about acts of government, in other words of the political control of the highway, aiming precisely at limiting the extraordinary power of assault that the motorization of the masses creates" (51). Earlier in the century, the concentration of industrial technology into individual motorized locomotion had already revolutionized the battlefield in the figure of the *tank*, that "automotive fort" (78). These offered their commanders a new calculus of speed and movement. As if sailing across a smooth surface, the tank "extends war over an earth that disappears, crushed under the infinity of possible trajectories" (79). Virilio suggests these "battleships of earth" (79) should not be called "all-terrain," but "*sans-terrain*" in their obliteration of territorial impediment (78). Later with the Jeep (and more grotesquely the Hummer) the personal fortress would allow for the (largely pretentious) presumption of this power to the performance of the daily commute.[6] But vehicular prostheticization is not only automotive. Others are assimilated as surgical prosthetics, others as fashion. The long marches of soldiers across fields plowed by battle during World War I presented the problem of damaged feet, and gave rise to the practical science of Orthopedics, and the redesign of the pedestrian soldier's locomotive technology: his *shoes*. This accomplishment is amplified and embellished in the cultural imaginary for which the sports shoe becomes a vehicle of personal ambulatory and logistical excellence ("Just do it").

The Information Bunker and the Ubiquitous Front

Today *information is architecture by other means*, framing and contouring the relative motility of social intercourse. While the city remains a locus of this staging and dissimulation of security, it is supplanted by other network media that have assumed some of its traditional mandates. Now highly evolved species of de Fourcroy's *tableau poliometrique* proliferate on screens and surfaces in the form of the graphical user interfaces, narrating the affordances of the softwares they inscribe. But these GUI are not just diagrams of virtual action to be taken, they are also mechanisms through which a user's motivation is first framed and then realized in the network and on the world. Modes of representation that were once cartographic and diagrammatic are now instrumental and mediational.

As the diagram becomes an interface, when the map becomes the tool, personal, individual social action becomes more logistical. The subjective manipulation of virtual symbols becomes a structural form of agency in this (pre-formatted) landscape of proximate and immediate contact. Consider how the political function of the urban gateway or boulevard to centralize and coordinate traffic and attention has been augmented by web portals and search engines, interfaces to the vast exabytes of online data curated and mainstreamed for public accessibility. There the preferences of mobs are codified in the ranking of search results associated with potential words, places, and concepts. Search represents a new configuration of public tools with which to seek, browse, meander, and exchange files with others, to be proximate to others in your social networks. Not unlike cities themselves, Search is legislated by a shifting balance of demographic desires, share-holder interest, and State paranoia. Virilio writes, "The State's political power…is the polis, the police, in other words, highway surveillance" (39). Indeed many core innovations in Search technology are sponsored by security interests (state and otherwise) needing to meaningfully sift petabytes of "chatter" from which intelligence critical to securing the polis might be gleaned.

Newer Search software works by making the world itself into the operant interactive metaphor for the world itself. Google Earth's interactive map/search/data visualization software, borrowing its interface aesthetics from previous generations of satellite—image-based battlefield simulation suites, promises to further incorporate personal logistics of everyday life into the tropics of "intelligence." Its open API (application programming interface) also allows users to link Google Earth to other data streams, personal and public, furthering tipping the logic of its performance from that of a "map with interactive capabilities," toward that of a real "meta-interface" based on cartographic, diagrammatic metaphors.

Just as diagrams become interfaces, computation also transforms physical urban interfaces by making them in turn increasingly diagrammatic. "In all parts of the world...implanted at the edges of cities, highways or railways...[is a] whole apparatus that is only the reconstitution of the various parts of the fortress motor, with its flankings, its gorges, its shafts, its trenches, admission to and escape from portals, the whole primordial control of the masses by organisms of urban defense" (40). Of the masses of *things*, that is. Today the urban interfaces of material exchange between supply chains and demand chains include ports of entry, now refitted as computationally-intensive logistics parks, which serve as regional switching mechanisms for the routing of components and the formation of geographically distributed assemblies of producers and consumers. There is a dromological heaven in these. The United Arab Emirates currently plans a truly Modern city of the future in their own in Jebel Ali, the Dubai Logistics City, which hopes to dwarf the strategic centrality of competing hubs in Rotterdam, Singapore, Shanghai and elsewhere by providing seemingly endless acreage of sea-air and air-air multi-modal passenger and cargo services: "merge-in-transit, customization, postponement, packaging and labeling, and final assembly." Today our visionary architecture is designed not for the care and habitation of people, but as *a utopia of and for objects.*

Impure War and the Exceptional Accident

Virilio's history—and our present moment—is a profile of violence, of both binding and fissure. While Virilio begins with the literal, primordial bunker, he extends the economy of attrition to characterize Modernity itself. The bunker and its double, the *camp*, are the elemental spaces of this. The bunker is a concrete prophylactic, the camp is incarcerating. Both are hygienic, defensive. One is an architectural membrane against a hostile world, and one is an expulsion-by-enclosure of the Other from the normal performance of law. In their extreme forms, both spaces, even as they are often architecturally identical, are in their way zones of *pure logistics*. They are sites where the only compulsion is the execution of governance on a raw mass, mobilizing it, diagramming it. They are only ideal types, and the real world is full of spaces (factories, airports, warehouses, laboratories, jails, shipping ports, etc.) that are complex combinations of the bunker and the camp, switching from one the other, inverting exteriorization and interiorization moment by moment.

For Virilio, the accumulation of capital is a means to ensure security, not the inverse. He writes: "Bourgeois power is military even more than economic, but it relates most directly to the occult permanence of the state of siege, to the appearance of fortified towns, those 'great immobile machines' made in different ways" (36). The competitive and complicit energies of the masses are understood as possessing a permanent *poliorcetic* historical mission (conducting or resisting sieges), and their movements are governed by the immobile surfaces of city, resolved in a suspended state of soft siege. This slow, permanent war is itself a technology of glacial attrition and shared deterrence. The city is in essence a bunker, characterized by Virilio as a deliberate "reduction of power in favor of a better trajectory, life traded for survival" (85). The "front" of this "pure war" is everywhere and everything, both inside and outside of the "closed world" of the "society of control." The comprehensive enclosure of earthly territory under dromocratic supervision totalizes this soft siege as a condition of global social space. Today's "security environment" (a preferred catch-phrase of Rumsfeld's) is populated by a *Poliorcetics Lite*, in which the defense of common civilian passage from potential acts of violence is folded into *design criteria* for the dissuasion of both petty and grand crime.[7]

But to be sure, Virilio's core exhortation diverges from that offered by a "frictionless capitalism" and its ideologies of reflexive transparency and seamless control. Instead, he sees the cumulative destiny of dromological globalization as a successively violent, increasingly integrated history of *accidents*. This Ballardian depiction of technology suggests that the invention or adoption of a new technology is always also the invention and adoption of a new accident. The invention of the ocean liner is also the invention of its catastrophic sinking, the internal combustion engine is itself the invention of greenhouse gases, the discoveries of genomic science also bring with them the latent horrors of a "genetic bomb," and the comprehensive integration of personal social lives into information networks is also their inevitable crash, taking with them the very social bonds that they contain and mediate for us. Such solutions also increase the scale of our shared risk. Virilio's recent work focuses on what he calls the "integral accident which may someday becomes our habitat," a kind of global (terminal?) accident in which the comprehensiveness of dromological administration promises as well an inevitable, equally global calamity of dysfunction.[8]

There is also an accident contained in *theoretical* technologies, and in the absorption of Virilio's theory by the institutional positions it seems to criticize so fiercely. "I am studied in military academies," he tells Sylvère Lotringer in *Pure War*, and indeed he is. Like that of advertising strategists pouring over the works of Guy Debord, this is but one instance of theory itself performing as a kind of "accidental" conceptual avant-garde for the institutions it had hoped to undo by careful description. Perhaps the most direct and disquieting exemplar is Israeli Brigadier General Aviv Kokhavi, the IDF Paratroop commander, charged with leading attacks on and thereby "redesigning" Palestinian territories in Nablus and elsewhere. Kokhavi is also an avid reader of Deleuze and Guattari's theoretical technologies of deterritorialization, smooth/striated space, and nomadology. In his holster, their richly nuanced theories of emergent antagonisms become tactical technologies for a newly sophisticated apparatus of state violence and rhizomatic repression.[9] But aren't such inversions—both simulations and dissimulations—somehow already intrinsic to the dromological violence in question? Aren't these "accidents of theory" already artifacts of the inversions that fundamentally characterize such configurations of violence? Football simulates primordial territorial clan warfare, and the supporters of Red Star

Belgrade are quickly recast as the shock troops of Serbian sweeps through Bosnia. As for American Football, the Louisiana Superdome, site of the universal simulated siege of the Superbowl, becomes after Katrina the host of a real siege and the festering bodies of those displaced by a slow war of systemic neglect—one still broadcast with high ratings. Are such inversions, or "accidents" (including the consumption of Virilio's theory of the dromological accident becoming a form of "intelligence" for the tactical management of dromocracy) are not (just) the exceptions but also the *rule*?

In the years since the publication of *Speed and Politics*, there has developed a rich discourse around the political function of the "exception," and the architecture of the camp as a space of that exception. For Giorgio Agamben, the camp represents an extralegal territory, derived from its exceptional status as being both founded outside the normal juridical procedures of the State, and precisely through this exceptional character, embodying the State's sovereignty not only over laws, but over law and the authority that it realizes.[10] The logic of the camp exceeds the normative productive link of power and resistance, revealing the *exception* as the real nexus of sovereign authority. Slavoj Zizek writes, in discussing Bahktin, that "what most deeply holds together a community is not so much identification with the Law that regulates the community's 'normal' everyday rhythms, but rather identification with a specific form of transgression of the Law, of the Law's suspension..."[11]

Virilio's own theories of dromocracy and the modernity of accidents should be considered in relation to this discourse. He writes that "the precious lesson of the camp and the gulags has not been heeded, because it was erroneously presented not only as an ideological phenomenon, but also as a static one, an enclosure. Its absolute inhumanity is...the social bestiary of the immense biomass, proletariat subsumed under logistical demands" (98). In the camp, the administration of "bare life," of the metabolic vehicles of dromocratic modernity, is rendered in stark relief. There is also a softer repetition of this in the world's "special economic zones," those extralegal logistical archipelagos that weave the flows of global commerce, and mobilize a new normative order in their image. But again, for Virilio the lesson is not the pretentious self-image of hyperefficiency that such networks communicate, but rather the exception that remains within the exception itself: the accident. The accident-within-the-accident emerges from the *identification* with the exception that Zizek names, perhaps in ways that Virilio might not himself recognize. Terrorism, for example, as well as the "state of emergency" of counter-terrorism, is neither entirely complicit with a symmetry of resistance to the law, nor ever possibly entirely outside it, but instead makes its claims over the sovereign exception to the law's authority to author. This is also the crux of the wonderment and awe provoked by the event of catastrophic failure. It is not only horrific, it is mesmerizing, and because it is, the accident is also a critical source of solidarity, a binding exception that is the real condition of acceptance. The carnival of accidents is revealed as technology's own exceptional bacchanalia, staged at our expense and on our behalf.

Benjamin H. Bratton is a theorist and consultant based in Los Angeles. He teaches at SCI_Arc (The Southern California Institute of Architecture) and UCLA. www.bratton.info

Notes

1. Paul Virilio/Sylvère Lotringer, *Pure War*. Trans. Mark Polizzotti. New York: Semiotext(e), 1983.

2. Paul Virilio, "Architecture Principe," *AA Documents 3: The Function of the Oblique*, Architectural Association, London. 1996. P. 13.

3. P. 68 of the present edition. *Speed and Politics: An Essay on Dromology*. Semiotext(e), New York. Subsequent parenthetical quotations are from this same edition.

4. The term "software society" is developed further in a forthcoming essay co-authored by Lev Manovich and myself.

5. Gilles Palsky, *Des chiffres et des cartes, naissance et la cartographie quantitative francaise au XIXe siecle developpement*. (Memoires de la section de geographie No. 19). Paris: Comite des travaux historiques et scientifiques, 1996. (translated by Daniel J. Denis) Pp.51–52

6. These rolling gated communities provide a more direct identification with military purpose. During the first Gulf War, a common bumper sticker was "I Support the Troops," whereas the parade of post-9/11 Hummers says rather "I Am The Troops."

7. The "security environment" is populated by small and large architectures of control: from "sit-proof benches" (benches and sidewalk planters designed with uncomfortable barbs to prevent loitering and keep pedestrians moving,) to the locking of workers overnight into the Big Box emporiums where they restock shelves until morning. We are treated to invited competitions by major newspapers for the "architectural" design of the U.S./Mexico border, and the current conception of a "Freedom Tower" at the former site of the World Trade Center as a ponderous concrete fortification wrapped in semi-translucent glass—an enduringly disingenuous symbol of martial culture.

8. The notion of technology revealing itself most directly in its failure again links Virilio's critique to Heidegger's. See Virilio, *Unknown Quantity*, Fondation Cartier pour l'art contemporain. Thames & Hudson, 2003. P.25

9. Kokhavi is quoted by Eyal Weizman, "Several of the concepts in *A Thousand Plateaus* became instrumental for us...allowing us to explain contemporary situations in a way that we could not otherwise have explained them. It problematized our paradigms... Most important was the distinction they have pointed out between the concepts of 'smooth' and 'striated' space... In the IDF we now often use the term 'to smooth out space' when we want to refer to operation in a space as if it had no borders." Weizman, "Lethal Theory," *Log* 7, Winter/Spring 2006. P. 59.

10. Agamben recounts recent responses to that the "scandalous" discovery of correspondence between Walter Benjamin and fascist jurist, Carl Schmitt, on sovereignty and violence—another "accident of theory"—and argues that it is Benjamin who should be understood to have "infected" Schmitt's position. See Agamben, *State of Exception*. University of Chicago Press, 2005. Pp. 52–64.

11. Slavoj Zizek, *The Universal Exception*. New York: Continuum Press, 2006. P. 64.

Part 1

THE DROMOCRATIC REVOLUTION

I wouldn't want to be a survivor.

— Jean Mermoz

1

From Street Fight to State Right

The mass of individuals that the smallest military unit offers the eye, united in a common voyage.

— Clausewitz, 1806

IN EVERY REVOLUTION there is the paradoxical presence of circulation. Engels remarks in June 1848: "The first assemblies take place on the large boulevards, *where Parisian life circulates with the greatest intensity.*" Less than a century later, Weber says of the disappearance of Rosa Luxemburg and Karl Liebknecht (as if he were talking about the results of a car crash) that "they called to the streets, and the streets killed them." The masses are not a population, a society, but the multitude of passersby. The revolutionary contingent attains its ideal form not in the place of production, but in the street, where for a moment it stops being a cog in the technical machine and itself becomes a motor (machine of attack), in other words a *producer of speed.*

For the mass of unemployed, demobilized workers without an occupation, Paris is a tapestry of trajectories, a series of streets and avenues in which they roam, for the most part, with neither goal nor destination, subject to a police repression intended to control their wanderings. For the various revolutionary groups, as for the

Apaches and other shady populations of the city's outskirts, it will be less a matter, when the time comes, of occupying a given building than of *holding the streets*.[1] In 1931, during the National Socialists' struggle against the Marxist parties in Berlin, Joseph Goebbels notes, "Whoever can conquer the streets also conquers the State!"[2]

Can asphalt be a political territory? Is the bourgeois State and its power the street, or *in* the street? Are its potential force and expanse in the places of intense circulation, on the path of rapid transportation?

As Goebbels again writes about the battles for Berlin, "The ideal militant is the political combatant in the Brown Army as a *movement*...obeying a law that he sometimes doesn't even know, but that he could recite in his sleep... Thus we have set these fanatical beings *in motion*..."

He then scientifically compares the transcripts of his various speeches, made first in the provinces and then later in Berlin, and notices that the "amorphous sociological conglomerate" of the capital required the invention of a "new language for the masses": "The rhythm of the metropolis with its four million souls throbs like a burning wind through the declarations of propagandists... Here a new and modern language was spoken, one that has nothing to do with the archaic forms of so-called popular expression. This is the beginning of an original artistic style, the first form of expression to be truly *animated* and *galvanizing*."

Mob riots reform the mob (the original mob of hunter-raiders). To lead the bands of "lost soldiers" of the workers' army—its *dromomaniacs*[3]—that is, for the leader, to incite them, "lead them to the attack like a pack of dogs," as Saint-Just said. It means giving rhythm to the mobile mass's trajectory through vulgar stimulation, a polemical symphony, transmitted far and wide, from one to the other, polyphonic and multicolored like the road signals and traffic directions meant to accelerate the telescoping, the shock of the accident.[4] This is the ultimate goal of street demonstrations, of urban disorder. "Propaganda must be made directly by words and images, not by writing," states Goebbels, who was himself a great promoter of audiovisuals in Germany. Reading implies time for reflection, a slowing down that destroys the mass's dynamic efficiency. If a monument should be penetrated by the mob, it will be rapidly transformed into a place of passage, where everyone enters and exits, brings to and takes away. It's the free-for-all, plunder for plundering's sake, as we saw even in 1975 at the fall of Saigon.

All through history there has been an unspoken, unrecognized revolutionary wandering, the organization of a *first mass transportation*—which is nonetheless revolution itself. Thus the old conviction that "every revolution takes place in the city" comes from the city; the expression "dictatorship of the Paris Commune," used as far back as the events of 1789, should not suggest so much the classic opposition of city to country as that of stasis to circulation.

Despite convincing examinations of city maps, the city has not been recognized as first and foremost a human dwelling place penetrated by channels of rapid communication (river, road, coastline, railway). It seems we've forgotten that the street is only a road passing through an agglomeration, whereas every day laws on the "speed limit" within the city walls remind us of the continuity of displacement, of movement, that only the speed laws modulate. The city is but a stopover, a point on the synoptic path of a trajectory, the ancient military glacis, ridge road, frontier or riverbank, where the spectator's glance and the vehicle's speed of displacement were instrumentally linked. As I have said in the past, there is only *habitable circulation*.[5]

This is particularly evident today in Japan—for example, in those immense revolutionary battles that come down to simple collision, to the provocation of a clash with the urban police, in which the mass of overtrained militants is armed with audio visual machines: movie cameras, tape recorders, etc. Aware of the kinetic nature of their actions, it's the instantaneousness of their presence (in the next second they have vanished from the street that they film and record); they, the passers-by for whom the ban on loitering goes hand in hand with the ban on gathering. In the same way they evaded the very revelatory slogan of the 1848 insurgents: "Desperate masses," writes Engels, "who demand bread and work, or death."

In fact, the watchword of these "workers' battalions" (as those who would be deported by force to the provinces or drafted into the army were called) was "*we're stayin'*"... we're not moving from here! The socialist utopia of the nineteenth century, like the democratic utopia of the ancient agora, was literally buried under the vast scaffolding of urban construction, obscuring the fundamental anthropological side of revolution, of proletarianization: the migratory phenomenon.

On September 21, 1788, Arthur Young notes in his famous journal: "...the great commercial city of Nantes!... Arrive—go to the theatre, new built of fine white stone. It was Sunday, and therefore full. *Mon Dieu!* cried I to myself, do all the wastes, the deserts, the heath, ling, furz, broom, and bog, that I have passed for 300 miles, lead to this spectacle?... There are no gentle transitions from ease to comfort, from comfort to wealth: you pass at once from beggary to profusion,—from misery in mud cabins to splendid spectacles at 500 liv. a night."

The new city with its riches, its unheard-of technical facilities, its universities and museums, its stores and permanent holidays, its comforts, its knowledge and its security, seemed an ideal spot for the tiring journey to end, the ultimate landing dock for the mass's migrations and hopes after a perilous crossing—so much so that until recently we confused urban and urbane for a place of social and cultural exchanges what was only a highway or railway exchanger. We took the crossroad for the path of socialism.

If municipalities rent out space at top dollar and slap surcharges on windows and street-side facades, it's because all these architectural details of the bourgeois dwelling traditionally carry the possibility of commerce and information. The display windows of Dutch prostitutes still reproduce today the old "bow windows" whose curvature allowed one a panoramic view of what was coming and going. The spectacle of the street is traffic, the "pilgrim's progress" movement of progression, of procession—at once voyage and improvement, a movement likened to progress toward something better, a pilgrimage that dominated the Middle Ages.[6] The street is like a new coastline and the dwelling a sea-port from which one can measure the magnitude of the social flow, predict its overflowings. The doors to the city are its tollbooths and its customs posts are dams, filtering the fluidity of the masses, the penetrating power of the migrating hordes. The old, swampy, unhealthy beaches that surrounded the fortified city, the "congo-plains" of the American slave, the old fortifications, the outskirts, the shantytowns and favellas—but also the poorhouse, the barracks, the prisons—solve a problem less of enclosure or exclusion than of traffic. All of them are uncertain places because they are situated between two speeds of transit, acting as brakes against the acceleration of penetration. Located from the outset on paths of terrestrial or fluvial communication, they will later be compared to sewers, to stagnant waters, the end of fluidity (progress), the sudden absence of motivity, ineluctably creating a quasi-organic corruption of the masses.

"Neutral spaces, spaces without genre," writes Balzac, "where every vice, every misfortune in Paris takes refuge." This is the origin of the sub-urb, at once the province of interdiction and a linear and temporal distance—in other words, the depot and "trans-shipment" of the social matter as of the merchandise, provisions and livestock to which the "beery" proletariat has been likened for centuries: essentially wild animals become beasts of burden, warhorses or pack animals. The conditions of the proletarian masses' exploitation, furthermore, illustrate perfectly the definition that Geoffroy Saint Hilaire gives of domestication: "To domesticate an animal is to accustom it to living and breeding in or near men's dwellings."

The "right to lodging" is not, as was claimed, the "right to enter the city." Like the inorganic mass of wild animals, the proletarian horde carries a menace, a load of unpredictability and ferocity. It is allowed as "domestic" to gather and reproduce near the dwellings of men, under their watchful eye. The problems of human *habitation* properly speaking are absolutely differentiated from those of the proletarian cattle, of its *lodgings* in the barnyard of the castle, in the outskirts of the fortified city. As with the stable or enclosure, the temporary lodging of the migrating masses implies their relative distance from the dwellings of men, in other words from the city. The bourgeoisie will get its initial power and class characteristics (which, of course, were not at all peculiar to them; we all know the capital role played by monasticism, chivalry, etc., in the areas of banking, industry...) less from commerce and industry than from *the strategic implantation that establishes the "fixed domicile" as a social and monetary value*[7]—from real estate speculation as the sale and trading of fixed property, the right to reside within the ramparts of fortified cities, the right to security and preservation within the perilous migration of a world of pilgrims, barges, soldiers and exiles moving onward by the millions.

Starting in 1077 with the Commune of Cambrai, the "urban franchises" will spread little by little to every commercial city. We could easily spot them on a map: logically, they are all situated on large waterways or highways, while regions difficult to reach such as Brittany or the Massif Central have few or no communes. The advent of bourgeois power with the revolution of the communes can already be likened to a "national war of liberation" since it sets, on its terrain, a native population against a military occupier come from the East who claims to govern its conquest. The guarantee of urban franchises is first and foremost the reorganization of the old Gallo-Roman site following the layout of the fortified castle, the construction of those impregnable fortresses that had nothing to fear from the war machines then in use, but everything to fear, at every moment, from surprises and strategems come from without, from afar, with the nomadic masses.

If the reorganization of the old villa, its transformation by the feudal colonizer into a castle replete with moat, set up stockades and dirt embankments against every natural danger and scourge without distinction, the architecture of the fortified castle that succeeded it lost this rural character and became purely military. From then on it addressed only one enemy: the man of war. Furthermore, what differentiates the ancient fortress from that of the Middle Ages in Europe, despite their apparent similarity, is that the latter, thanks to the architectural organization of its internal spaces, *allows one to prolong combat indefinitely*, with its slits, its projections, its trenches, its high walls...[8] The fortified enclosure of the Middle Ages creates an artificial field, makes this field *a stage* on which physical and psychological constraints can be imposed. After Machiavelli, Vauban will heartily support this means of *avoiding carnage* and of *breaking up the enemy* simply by constructing a topological universe made of "a totality of mechanisms able to receive a defined form of energy (in this case, that of the mobile mass of assailants), *to transform it and finally to return it in a more appropriate form.*"

Reorganized according to the same principle, the communal fortress remaines a "field of strategems" set for the adversary. But the latter changes character once more, becoming first and foremost a social enemy.

Aside from its military function, the rampart of the fortified place assumes a class function; its poliorcetic conception allows it to prolong the social combat indefinitely. The communal bourgeoisie gives rise to a new phenomenon, like a prolonged and patient war that has all the earmarks of the inertia of peace, and nothing more of the bloody effusions of ancient civil war, the seasonal outbursts and violent movements of the country battlefield. Bourgeois power is military even more than economic, but it relates most directly to the occult permanence of the state of siege, to the appearance of fortified towns, those "*great immobile machines made in different ways.*"[9] In the same way, the decadence of the enclaved bourgeoisie, the loss of its own will, will be linked to the decline of its military technique in the domain of ground warfare. As Montesquieu remarks, "With the invention of gunpowder, the impregnable place ceased to exist."

Clausewitz has admirably shown the mercenaries of the large Italian cities, then of Europe in general, lending their services to powerful economies—the only ones capable of furnishing the military entrepreneur with an increasingly large budget, the goods and transferable holdings that he can take with him at the end of his engagement contract (whence the "evident conjuncture between money and *what seems* to found it, its military significance"—Marx to Engels, September 25, 1857). But he doesn't go far enough in designating the latter as technical manufacturer, as engineer (of weapons). In fact, it was the military engineers who, depending on the opportunities afforded, were able to protect or destroy private securities within the bourgeois citadel. And here we have the unspoken conjucture from which the "cannibalistic classes" will come—not only the bourgeoisie, but also the permanent military class. The Marxist definition of capitalism, "consumer of human life and founder of dead labor," is quite apt for the bourgeoisie, but only insofar as it is associated with its military technical adviser, who simultaneously invents the means of producing and of destroying what he produces, a war entrepreneur who will be at the origin of the State armies and later of the military industrial complex. Just as the *condottiere* had benefited from this system of ruin by leaning on the city's economic orientation, so the communal bourgeoisie already carries within itself the same ambiguous association of wealth and the production of destruction.

This fatal merger was formed on these grounds like a chance meeting: "The strategic importance of a given proposition is not the result of largely hypothetical combinations, but of the very configuration of the countryside: this will be an important knot of communication lines, the meeting point of numerous roads or the confluence of valleys." As we saw before, wherever these conditions are fulfilled, there are population centers; where there is traffic, there is also the urban area. To recapitulate, the conditions that obtained at the birth of the great cities are always those that make these cities important strategic points.[10] The solution, then, imposed itself, and *up until the twentieth century* they almost always decided to transform the most populous centers into large fortresses. National Defense continued to mix, in almost medieval fashion, military men with the civilians whose resources (supplies, physical labor, lodgings, arms, etc.) were of no small importance to the army. The very givens of capitalism, the inactivity of its wealth, directly contribute toward maintaining the state of siege!

If the fortified town is an immobile machine, the military engineers specific task is to fight against its inertia. "The goal of fortification is not to stop armies, to contain them, *but to dominate, even to facilitate their movements.*" Around 1870 Colonel Delair notes: "Every fortress must possess a certain particular state, a certain power of resistance, which in men is called *good health.* In peacetime, we officers of the engineering corps are responsible for keeping the fortress in good health." And a bit further on: "The art of defense must constantly be in transformation; it is not exempt from the general law of this world: *stasis is death.*"[11]

The communal fortress is a city machine, so much so that Cormontaigne, Fourcroy and many engineers of the eighteenth century, in their "fictional diaries of sieges" or their "moments of fortification," don't even mention the troops assigned to defend it, as if the fortress were capable of functioning by itself. General de Villemoisy in the nineteenth century notes its technical superiority: "Out of 300 sieges conducted by the Europeans since the beginning of this century, there have only been about ten in which the fortification fell first." The military thus seems dependent on the general concept of the fortified place. Carnot praises its division of labor: "It has been proven that bravery and industry—which, taken separately, would not suffice—can, once they are joined, multiply each other." After Vauban, the defenders' presence in the fortified place will not be a matter of chance: the decree of December 28, 1866, will still name the governors of fortified cities as permanent residents in both peace and war, just as the garrison will be obliged to perform daily tasks, each one being assigned a fixed and invariable function, repeated day after day.

The occupants of the Maginot Line, for their part, had gotten into the habit of calling it "the factory." Long after the dismantling of the old communal city and up until the twentieth century, when large fortified places still exist, the military class continues to find work with its old bourgeois employer, the two slowly becoming "compradores." The interests of the war entrepreneur remain aligned with those of capitalism in permanent strategic schemas: in 1793, Barere compares the young Republic (the Paris Commune) *to a large city under siege* and he calls for *all of France to be no more than a vast camp*. The political triumph of the bourgeois revolution consists in spreading the state of siege of the communal city machine, immobile in the middle of its logistic glacis and domestic lodgings, over the totality of the national territory. And in 1795, it will entrust to Carnot's new armies the job of pushing as far back as possible the assault by the popular masses come from the suburb, of encircling the Faubourg Saint-Antoine, of forcing the dismayed workers to give up their weapons to its 20,000 soldiers "who had forgotten that they were also of the people" (Babeuf).

The State's political power, therefore, is only secondarily "power organized by one class to oppress another." More materially, *it is the polis, the police, in other words highway surveillance*, insofar as, since the dawn of the bourgeois revolution, the political discourse has been no more than a series of more or less conscious repetitions of the old communal poliorcetics, confusing social order with the control of traffic (of people, of goods), and revolution, revolt, with traffic jams, illegal parking, multiple crashes, collisions. The results of the 1977 French municipal elections were exemplary in this respect, since they reinscribed, on the national territory, Barere's old plan to cut France in two: at the center the decisive knot of the capital where the right triumphs, and all around the *vast camp* of the suburbs and provinces that voted for the left because they were conscious of becoming a hinterland in which productive activity was on the decline. On the other hand, these elections also show how much the opposing party's discourse is dominated by the reactionary schema of bourgeois poliorcetics, confining the mass's ability to move with its ability to attack—the *ultreia* of pilgrim's progress. But beyond that, this political police schema, accepted until very recently by every ideology, influences both urban and worldwide planning; the passage from the "great immobile machine" to the State-machine, and finally to the planet machine, is accomplished without difficulty. The words "politics of progress" or "of change" are devoid of meaning if, behind the electric megalopolis, the city knows no rest, if we can't distinguish the obscure silhouette of the old fortress struggling against its inertia, for whom stasis is death.

In all parts of the world, social lodgings, the city-dormitory or port of transit, implanted at the edges of cities, highways or railways, the toll systems that the government insists so strongly on instituting at the very entrances to a capital that selection is depopulating, the general police headquarters set up right nearby—this whole apparatus is only the reconstitution of the various parts of the fortress motor, with its flankings, its gorges, its shafts, its trenches, admission to and escape from its portals, the whole primordial control of the masses by the organisms of urban defense.

We also saw, during the German occupation of France, how easy it was for pseudo-social lodgings in the suburbs (Drancy, for example), like the old poorhouse, to be transformed into pivots toward the "beyond" of other voyages, other deportations. Whatever their supposed ideology, the proper role of every totalitarian regime is to bring to the fore the mitigated role of the army and the police (v. their rivalry) vis a vis the unrecognized order of *political circulation.* We could even say that the rise of totalitarianism goes hand-in-hand with the development of the state's hold over the circulation of the masses. Because of this, from the outset, it is easy to spot in the history of the great administrative bodies of the State: it was Sully, himself a grand master of roads and canals, who brought "the administration of fortifications" out of the rut with the edict of 1604 and gave it a modern form which continued well into the twentieth century, despite apparent revolutions.

As Tocqueville remarks, *the quartermasters of fortifications simultaneously perform, in the most ambiguous fashion, the state's civilian and military duties.* Under Louis XIV, Mesrine will be assigned to create permanent companies of miners, sappers and boatmen who will originally be *part of the corps of engineers*, and who will replace the volunteer engineers—labor inspectors come up from the ranks or civilian public works officials, such as the famous Tarade, who was also in charge of Parisian sanitary engineering. Thus, on the eve of the bourgeois revolution of '89, the Army Corps of Engineers was providentially given a national task: not only the construction/destruction of the urban ramparts, but also the expansion of the logistical glacis over the whole territory (Barere's "vast camp of the nation").

Thus we shouldn't wonder about the exceptional vogue of engineers after the seventeenth century, a vogue that in the nineteenth century would become a veritable cult in philosophy and fiction. The engineer is celebrated as the "priest of civilization" (Saint-Simon), a perverted image we will come back to, but which appears quite naturally after that of the "castrameter"—the latter really a priest or man of the Church assigned to teach "the art of limiting camps and fortified places by geometrical layouts." (But already, as Colonel Lazard noted, it was no longer a question of a *specifically* military art, but rather a kind of reign of descriptive geometry projected onto the sites, *over the totality of nature*...)[12] *The military class* is not born of the overpopulated headquarters of the *ancien régime*, offices in which one saw marshals and general officers alternate, almost daily, the command of the traditional armies. Under such conditions—even if they had considerable budgets at their disposal —there was little danger that these armies could demonstrate any kind of unified thought or strategic imagination. The only military activity that requires continuity of ideas, then, is the logistical project of the urban fortress. And it's from this equivocal logistical duty that the mixture of combat planning and territorial layout, christened "National Defense" by the bourgeois revolution, is born.

Vauban is the precursor here. An avid reader of Vitruvius and obsessed by the Roman colonial model, he thinks that the basis of war is geo-political and universal, that human geography should depend not on chance but on organizational techniques able to control fairly vast spaces, fairly durable empires. Aside from the old highway maintenance, this new military thought incorporated economic forecasts, genetic concerns, problems of food, etc. It is again an engineer and director of fortifications, of course, who in 1782 will publish *one of the first known flowcharts*: Charles de Fourcroy and his "Sketch for a poleometric table or the musings of a diagram lover on the magnitude of several cities with a map or chart offering a comparison of these cities in the same scale." This is the first "two-way" map, a contemporary of the scientific map of France by the Cassinis.

This military thought, that claims by functional planning to eliminate chance (which it considers synonymous with disaster and ruin), becomes totally confused at the end of the *ancien régime* with the thinking of the bourgeois political class, its taste for rational nomenclature, its tireless activity of totalitarian scribe (encyclopedist), the osmosis taking place at the entrance to the cities (permeable membrane between the highway and the street). The head of the first Parisian municipality was, as we know, the director of the Hanse.[13] The City Hall overlooked the waterfront, and the boat has remained the vehicular emblem of what was no more than a nauta-city. The same preoccupations reappear toward 1749 in the works of police officer Guillaute, for example: "No more revolts, no more seizures, no more tumults," he writes. "Public order will reign if we are careful to distribute our human time and space between the city and the country by a severe regulation of transit; if we are attentive to schedules as well as to alignments and signal systems; if by environmental standardization the entire city is made transparent, that is, familiar to the policeman's eye."

Today many people are discovering, somewhat late in the game, that once the "first public transport" of the revolution has passed, socialism suddenly empties of its contents—except, perhaps, military (national defense) and police (security, incrimination, detention camps).

The time has come, it seems, to face the facts: revolution is movement, but movement is not a revolution. Politics is only a gear shift, and revolution only its overdrive: war as "*continuation* of politics by other means" would be instead a police *pursuit* at greater speed, with other vehicles. The *ultima ratio* very carefully engraved on pieces of artillery under Louis XIV expressed quite well the procedure for changing speed. The piece of artillery is a mixed vehicle that synthesizes two velocities of displacement: that of the relatively rapid tractor-drawn cannon, and the lightning speed of the projectile toward its explosion as the ultimate argument of reason. In the same way, "political socialism," by its *political nature* (polis), usually fails when the acceleration of civil war toward urban collision stops, itself being nothing other than…

Some regard unfavorably the current proliferation of parades in the city, ambulatory manifestations, even a "rally of the unemployed," such as in April 1977 in Thionville. They don't really see, after the sporting grand finale of May '68, the professional or social effectiveness of such performances. Nonetheless, these urban cross-country races, these obstacle courses, have a precise goal that the classics of western revolutionary culture, such as *Pravda*, again revealed in the summer of 1976: "Parading in the streets is a worker's best possible preparation for the battle for power…"

Already under the *ancien régime*—the monarch's physical person being associated with the State—we see disturbances, scenes of revolt as soon as the king's place of residence becomes uncertain. The Parisian populace penetrates the Royal Palace; then, after having been admitted to contemplate the sovereign, leaves feeling calmer. In the same way, for the proletarian masses from the country or the suburbs, the simple fact of penetrating to the heart of Paris, of feeling under their feet its avenues and opulent streets, is a very concrete way of diminishing a real and measurable social and political resistance between the masses and the constructed power of the bourgeois State. In fact, mass movements under the *ancien régime*, wandering in search of the person of the monarch/State, prefigure the new organization of traffic flows that we arbitrarily call the "French Revolution," which is nothing other than the rational organization of a social abduction. The "mass uprising" of 1793 is *the removal of the masses.*

The discourse propagated by revolutionary propaganda is like the bourgeois citadel's old religious discourse. It distances and dissuades the mobile masses; it designates a new revolutionary State as not being here in the city, in the streets, but over there, far away, in the excessiveness of a universal and timeless raid. "Embrace," cries Gregoire, "the expansion of the centuries as that of the regions...avoid a much-heeded prejudice that would circumscribe the Republic in a very restricted territory!" (November 27, 1792)—while the bourgeoisie immediately gives itself new properties and estates, and threatens with death all who would question the right to private property (March 18, 1793). What it offers *as territories to its "conscripts" are the roads of Europe.* "Where the feet are, there is the fatherland" (*ubi pedes, ibi patria*), Roman law had already decreed. With the French Revolution, *all the highways became national*!

The movement of the Parisian *sans-culottes* preceded the "mass uprising" of '93 as, much later, the sinister adventure of Hilter's "Brown Shirts," the *Sturmabteilung*, would precede the German mobilization for total war. Like them, the *sans-culottes* are dromomaniacs, "couriers of terror" sent forward before the Revolution onto the Parisian pavement. The decree of March 21, 1793, legalizes their specific function: *these militant political fanatics are only the logistical agents of terror, members of the "police"*: denunciation of "suspects," surveillance of neighborhoods and buildings, deliverance of certificates of civic merit, arrests, but also provisions, circulation and navigation of commodities, price controls...

In May they will be absorbed into the Army of the Interior, sent in infernal columns along the roads of the provinces. One year later their leaders will be executed, like the supreme commander of the Brown Shirts on June 30, 1934, the "Night of the Long Knives."

Revolution is no more than a rerouting of the old social assault. Carnot, as a good member of the Corps of Engineers, channels his fleet far from the communal fortress, toward the "army zones." He still prefers to take his contingents from the Parisian popular forces; the soldier of Year II is torn from the street that he wanted to conquer and involved in the irrational voyage, the deportation of the long and murderous "forced march." "The new army," writes Carnot, "is a mass army *crushing the adversary under its weight* in a *permanent offensive*, to the tune of the *Marseillaise*." The national anthem is only a road song, regulating the mechanics of the march. In his memoirs, Poumies de la Siboutie notes, "Never had we sung so much...*songs were a powerful revolutionary means, the 'Marseillaise' electrified the populace...*"

The mathematician Carnot and the doctor Poumies were not mistaken: the revolutionary song is a kinetic energy that pushes the masses toward the battlefield, toward the kind of Assault that Shakespeare had already described as "Death killing Death." And that is in fact what it is all about, since one had to charge the enemy artillery, and the only way was for the infantryman to rush toward the cannons, to kill its servants on the spot. But to reach them, he had an extremely limited amount of time: the time it took the enemy artillery to reload. As soon as the shot had been fired, therefore, the infantryman had to rush toward the enemy cannons. His life then depended on his running speed; if he was too slow, he died literally disintegrated point blank by the firing end...

Everything in this new warfare becomes a question of time won by man over the fatal projectiles toward which his path throws him. Speed is Time saved in the most absolute sense of the word, since it becomes human Time directly torn from Death—whence those macabre emblems of decimation worn down through history by the Assault troops, in other words the *rapid troops* (black uniforms and flags, death's heads, by the uhlan, the SS, etc.).

But beyond this, what should we think of this revolution that will soon be entirely reduced to a permanent Assault on Time? The perpetual offensive of Carnot's mass armies is the reversal of the old "run before you." Salvation is no longer in flight; safety is in "running toward your Death," in "killing your Death." *Safety is in Assault* simply because the new ballistic vehicles make flight useless; they go faster and farther than the soldier, they catch up with him and pass him. The man on the battlefield has no safety, it seems, other than in a suicidal entrance into the very trajectory of the speed of the engines. It is toward this that he is pitilessly pushed by the new military jurisdiction that takes him literally "between two fires!" *From now on, general safety can come only from the masses in their entirety reaching speed.* Napoleon expresses it clearly: "Aptitude for war is aptitude for movement," and he specifies that one must evaluate the strength of the army "as in mechanics, by its mass multiplied by its speed."

Hegel, admiring the French revolutionaries, writes in January 1807 to a friend: "Every Frenchman has learned to look Death in the face." In particular, he compares the old institutions to "those children's shoes, become too tight, *that hinder the gait*, and that the revolutionaries soon got rid of." Always the unconscious dynamic metaphor, the new dialectics of the battlefield transcribed in philosophical and political terms. The under-equipped French soldier, actually looks his Death in the face—in the black, gaping hole of the cannon toward which he throws himself. This "army of dwarves" (Goethe) would need "seven-league boots": "a troop of dwarves, when we expected to see giants in Germany." But this was understandable, since their probable size had been calculated *on the basis of their road speed.* The Germans had imagined long strides taken by huge individuals. They hadn't counted on the new factor:

the inordinate development of the kinetic energy of the revolutionary masses. This discourse likens the acquisition of high speeds of assault, of invasion, even of explosion, to the "mechanics" of a revolution symbolized primarily by the conquest of the streets, then "liberating" itself on the highway.

Significantly, every totalitarian combat will repeat this procedure. The German National Socialists, enemies of the bourgeoisie—or at least claiming to be in order to *mobilize* the dromomaniacs of the Brown Shirts—take over the German State, city by city, or rather street by street, before spreading highway by highway toward the neighboring territories, as if the German masses, "set in motion" by their leaders' *dynamic declarations*, could no longer be stopped.

After the conquest of the streets and the massacre of the Brown Shirts, the National Socialist motor will nonetheless come back to its ordinary drivers: the lower- and middle-class administrators; the big capitalism that, since the 1920s, had furnished it with important subsidies; the Reichswehr and the vehicles of Rommel and Guderian, carrying the military front far off, "where the tanks are." With the National Socialist lightning-war, the old, outmoded frontier wall disappears, ostensibly replaced by the rapid path. Already, the German nation is no longer exactly where its famous boots—the symbol of its army—fall, but rather under the tracks of its tanks, in the motor force of its "steel front." As Ratzel wrote at the end of the nineteenth century, "War consists in advancing your boundaries over the other's territory." *The front is now no more than a war isobar reviving ancient rites of foundation.* But for the dromocrat of total war, the once-so-coveted city is already no longer in the city. Warsaw, archaically declared an "open city," is destroyed in September by air raids.

2

From Highway Right to State Right

The attack changed with the invention of machines to destroy.

— Errard, known as Bar le Duc

AS SOON AS it takes power, the Nazi government offers the German proletariat sport and transport. No more riots, no need for much repression; to empty the streets, it's enough to promise everyone the highway. This is the "political" aim of the Volkswagen, a veritable plebiscite, since Hitler convinced 170,000 citizens to buy a VW when there still wasn't a single one available. The "NSKK" (*National Socialistisches Kraftfahr Korps*: the National Socialist automobile corps) is organized locally, according to the categories of privately-owned cars. It soon gathers half a million drivers and trains them to drive over every kind of terrain, to shoot while driving, etc. Every member of these "sporting" clubs thus returns, in this exercise, to the premonitory techniques of Bonnot's and Al Capone's vehicular crimes. But if it is true that in 1941 Brecht, in *The Resistable Ascent of Arturo Ui,* was content to make a gangster Hitler's double, the similarities nonetheless go beyond simple parody. The American migrant's race to power is, like the fascist tragedy or the anarchistic adventure of Bonnot in 1911, inseparable from the revolution in transportation. Like Mussolini and Hitler, the great figures of American gangsterism begin in the street where they wander as beggars, as foreigners—the famous Jim Colosimo began as a streetsweeper and, like many of his compatriots, naturally passed over the threshold of the political shop as an electoral agent, a door-to-door salesman.

Later, the municipalities remain under the influence of the "brown troop" of their S.A. for, there as well, the automobile apotheosis of the 1920s, with its kidnappings, its shootings, its street battles, the wild chases of its armored cars, is but a technical episode in the dromocratic assault on the city and its wealth by a migrant mass come from Europe or Asia—before it becomes the Assault on the American State itself. But wasn't Al Capone supported on the national scale by the Republican Party? And didn't he owe his "training" to his voluntary service in the U.S. Army?

The unknown troops of gangsters will furthermore be spotlighted during the last war at the time of the Italian liberation, and its men revealed as "good American citizens."

On another level, we can understand how the American government will survive the economic crisis of the 1930s and cure the masses of their "temptation of the streets." Here as well the experience of the gangster-dromocrats is fairly instructive. The stroke of genius will consist in doing away with the direct repression of riots, and the political discourse itself, by unveiling the essence of this discourse: the transportation capacity created by the mass production of automobiles (since 1914 with Ford) can become a social assault, a revolution sufficient and able to modify the citizen's way of life by transforming all the consumer's needs, by totally remodeling a territory that (need we be reminded of it?) at the beginning had no more than 400 kilometers of road.

Doctor Helmut Klotz notes in 1937 that "the National Socialist Automobile Corps is an organization that, within strict boundaries, could immediately become useful to the motorization of the German Army." If he thinks that motorization presents only a limited advantage over long distances, he nonetheless recognizes that over a short distance it has *the power to increase the Assault Forces' strength to an extraordinary degree.*

On the shores across the way, the perpetual transformation of the barbarous esthetic of the mass-produced American car, the provocative excess of its body, of its ornaments, manifest the permanence of the social revolution (progress toward the "American way of life"). But at the same time, this great automobile body has been emasculated, its road holding is defective and its powerful motor is bridled. Just as for the laws on speed limits, we are talking about acts of government, in other words of the political control of the highway, aiming precisely at limiting the "extraordinary power of assault" that motorization of the masses creates.

This frustration inflicted on the driver (who is suddenly deprived of the "high" of high speeds as he is of alcohol), this vehicular prohibition is also the constitution by the State of a new beyond: "There were literally millions of youngsters who could drive cars, or repair them, who could build their own radio sets and communicate as 'hams' all over the world (experts in cross-country motorcycle and circulation), a whole generation of competent resourceful mechanics and electricians," remarks V. Bush in 1949 in *Modern Arms and Free Men.* "Every corner garage, every radio club, was a sort of center of training, training that could be readily transformed in a short time, when the test came, into the ability to operate the complex implements of war."

This permanent exploitation of the ignorant masses' aptitude for movement as a *social solution* is not peculiar to industrialized nations. The problem of shoes had been posed to civilian industry by the mass armies before that of cars. In 1792 the Supply Corps are able to furnish the barefoot troops with 200 pairs of shoes, when they would need 80,000.[1] Nonetheless, since "walking is a strategic instrument even apart from military engagement," as we saw, this kind of Assault is, first launched against Time and can be realized *theoretically* even when the material means are lacking.

Currently, the opposition parties are fighting about the "transportation time" of the workers. Here again, it's a question of "time saved," and we return to the origins of social "metamorphosis." We are here at the level of the "revolution of three eights" so dear to the men of 1848—eight hours of work, eight of sleep, eight of leisure time. A more remarkable fact is that this demand, when it is made, has from the outset had the singular merit of *creating unity* between all the parties, in every revolutionary movement, from the moderates to the extremists. This "time war" waged by the workers "has all the advantages of a revolutionary demand without any of the drawbacks."[2] Thus the Soviet republic decides to introduce it in autumn 1917, and the German republic in 1918.

The French republic, at the end of the war, fears a bloody May 1. And in fact, for that day in 1919, an enormous parade is again being organized, and the government knows that the only watchword will be "eight hours." But hadn't the Socialist Party heads just distinguished themselves in the responsibilities of power? Hadn't one of them headed the Ministry of Weapons? To grant the "eight hours" was thus to "preserve a definitive seal, *to keep in peacetime what had existed in wartime: a sacred bond.*"

On May 1, 1919, the proletariat is again demobilized; it has just left the glacis of the trenches and once more finds itself "facing death" in the glacis of the city streets. After the hugs and kisses of the first days, what was taken for civilian "ingratitude" toward the front lines is only a return to normalcy, to the citizen's basic distrust of and disdain for the masses of gyrovagues regaining their freedom of movement, again becoming available for the political battle...

In 1936 the true nature of these "eight hours of leisure," which has until then remained mysterious, is revealed: leisure means paid vacation, and paid vacation means travel—even the "last voyage," as was strangely underlined by a famous song of the so-called euphoric Popular Front. A revolution in transportation, not in happiness—toward campsites, youth hostel/barracks; camps everywhere, the great camp of territory. But isn't the Spanish Civil War about to be declared, and French non-intervention to become the tomb of the Popular Front that stops dead by refusing the "beyond" of this final voyage?

The abusive manipulation of the dromocratic discourse by the men of the political bourgeoisie should have warned us long ago about their true revolutionary intentions.

The events of 1789 claimed to be a revolt against *subjection*, that is, against the *constraint to immobility* symbolized by the ancient feudal serfdom (which furthermore persisted in certain regions)—a revolt against arbitrary confinement and the obligation to reside in one place. But no one yet suspected that the "conquest of the freedom to come and go" so dear to Montaigne could, by a sleight of hand, become an *obligation to mobility*. The "mass uprising" of 1793 was the institution of the first *dictatorship of movement*, subtly replacing the *freedom of movement* of the early days of the revolution.

The reality of power in this first modern State appears beyond the accumulation of violence as an accumulation of movement. In short, on July 14, 1789, the taking of the Bastille was a truly *Foucaldian* error on the part of the people of Paris: *the famous symbol of imprisonment is already an empty fortress*, the rioters discovering with astonishment that there's no one left to "liberate" behind its formidable walls.

The strategic schema of the revolution gives the two dominating classes their specific proletariat: the "nation on the march" of the mass army's military proletariat sent out on the "highway territory," and an industrial proletariat, a "worker's army," as it is called, that remains enclosed in the *vast camp* of the national territory. We can thus clearly distinguish two functions (or rather, functionings) of the thus-mobilized proletarian base, for never were the terms of proletarianization more radically set than by the Convention in its decree of February 1793: "The young shall go to war," while "married men, women and children will be forced to work in manufacturing" (arms, clothing, tents, bandages, etc.)—in short, logistical provisions. We see, then, that the new commercial bourgeoisie tends to enrich itself by amassing the *productive movements (actions)* of the industrial proletariat (the bourgeoisie of the Gironde and the war suppliers, the Swiss bank with Perregaux, etc.), while the military class amasses the *destructive act* of the mobile masses, and the *production of destruction* is accomplished by the proletariat's power of assault.

History shows that the decay of the enclosed bourgeoisies necessarily marks the decline of the productive masses and the rise in the State of methods of military proletarianization. In its doings, the Marxist State, for example, first appears as a *dictatorship of motor functions*, a totalitarianism very carefully programming and exploiting every form of *mass movement.* According to the rare witnesses, after the fall of Phnom Penh Cambodia becomes a "vast camp," and they rail against Marx and the Soviets as "inventors of the gulag"—whereas in reality it is only an outburst of the movement of military proletarianization. In fact, according to their own expression, the Khmer Rouges see the civilian populations of their own country, its millions of men, women and children, as "prisoners of war." The new leaders of Cambodia apply—to the letter, it seems—a memoir left twenty-five years earlier to the Sorbonne by Kieu Samphan. Thus we know where the virus that is ravaging this unfortunate country comes from: the utopian schema of the Cambodian revolution is only the antithesis of the bourgeois revolution. The large cities were brutally emptied of their inhabitants, who were massacred or thrown out into the countryside; certain neighborhoods were razed, replaced by rice fields; there is no communication between city and country; the only inhabitants of the depopulated city now are several infantry battalions, the Khmer leaders and certain diplomatic missions. More than a revolution, it's the tragic end of the siege on the communal fortress, finally submerged by its assailants.

In 'liberated" Vietnam, they discover other kinds of proletarian mobilization: after the fall of Saigon, certainly, a primary concern of the revolutionary armies was to put "unworthy" elements such as prostitutes or the lazy black market dealers of the great Southern city to work on logistical reconstruction (of strategic roads, railroads, bridges, etc.). But it was also to teach its youth, decked out in new uniforms, to "mime" its joy at being liberated—thus teaching it the simplicity of a power that comes down to the constraint and housebreaking of bodies. The dictatorship of the proletariat is only this dictatorship of movement (of the act) that is revealed by the great totalitarian holidays with their immense kinetic crowds. The *spartakiades* and gymnastic celebrations are always given a place of honor in the Eastern bloc countries, just as they were in the time of fascism: this synchronization integrates thousands of individuals into geometric ensembles as did, once upon a time, the square" of military maneuvers. The crowd's dynamism becomes a kaleidoscopic decoration, voluntarily forming slogans or gigantic portraits of the Party leaders, allowing the revolutionary militant to become for an instant a part of Mao's or Stalin's body.

But even more interesting are the rehabilitation camps which the Vietnamese, after the Chinese, are evidently so proud of, since they will supposedly eliminate from the system bloody repression and brutal punishment. These camps, to which they send men *without judgment,* should warn us by their very medical designation: rehabilitation has to do with the mechanical programming of invalid or handicapped bodies; it claims to *repair* them. The ideological delinquent or dissident is no longer considered a political opponent; he is not allowed the preferential psychiatric treatment accorded by the Russians or the Americans to their intellectuals. Materialism reaches its absolute form, since even the possiblity of granting importance to an opposing thought, to a differing concept, is totally eliminated. The dissident is a body, his dissidence a postural crime—for example, his indolence, his lasciviousness. Ostensibly, there are hardly any more crimes of opinion, only crimes of gesture. The confession is superceded: bodies are guilty of being out of synch, they have to be put back in the party *line,* at the speed of an entire population in maneuvers, for whom everything is an opportunity for public physical exercise, from the classic handling of arms to relaxation and gymnastics in the street, in the camps, in the factories, in team sports and dance, telluric and ecological guard duty, etc.[3]

During the Chinese cultural revolution, one often saw a kind of embarrassment on the faces of Mao and Chou En-lai before those millions of individuals brandishing, like so many robots, the "little red book." Was the revolution of civilization desired by the poet going to be reduced to this gymnastic group doubled by a mass denunciation campaign that was posted on the walls of Peking, like the Paris Commune one hundred years earlier (a police state, Cluseret called it), like the Cambodian revolution with its "kang-Chhlop?" Was socialism going to be reduced to a socialization of "intelligence?"

It is understandable that the *political* revolution ends up redistributing police functions (powers) to all the militants as if they were so many agents of the military highway patrol, harnessed under the *ancien régime* to the establishment of social transparency, to the observation of postures and movements not conforming to the social corpus—but also observation of the territorial body, as in telluric surveillance; a kind of ecological police that revives urban control, and seems for the powers that be to be a solution of the future.

Castro trading in his sloppy guerrilla garb for a uniform *á la* Pinochet, Brezhnev dressing up as a marshal, the massive presence of overdecorated military leaders in every socialist grandstand in the world tell us: the ultimate capitalizers on the productive act, the true dictators of movement—are them. It's from them, and not from vague philosophers or ideologues, that the political idea *of nations on the move* was born in 1789—the masses of the new military proletariat becoming *projectiles* toward the middle of the nineteenth century with the triumph of industrial artillery and the spread of machine warfare. "Heavy cannons," writes Trotsky in 1914, "instill in the working classes the idea that when you cannot get around an obstacle, you can still break through it; *the static phases of their psychology then give way to the dynamic phases.*"

After Lenin, Mao will qualify the people as the "motor force of history" when the importance of the conquest of energy sources arises. The political metaphor follows closely behind logistical progress to the extent that it claims a place in History. Military science, like History, is but a persistent perception of the kinetics of vanished bodies; inversely, bodies can appear as vehicles of history, as its dynamic vectors. Napoleon III claimed that "for the man of war, the ability to remember is science itself."

Part 2

DROMOLOGICAL PROGRESS

1

From Space Right to State Right

The creature bound by water is a creature in vertigo. It dies at each instant; something of its substance is constantly collapsing.
— Bachelard

AN ENGLISH CARTOON from the nineteenth century shows Bonaparte and Pitt cutting chunks out of an enormous globe-shaped pudding with their sabers, the Frenchman taking the continents while the Englishman claims the sea. This is another way of parceling out the universe: rather than confronting each other on the same terrain, within the limits of the battlefield, the adversaries choose to create a fundamental physical struggle between two types of humanity, one populating the land, the other the oceans. They invent nations that are no longer terrestrial, homelands in which no one could set foot; homelands that are no longer countries. The sea is open, the joining of the demos and the element of freedom (of movement). The "right to the sea," it seems, is a particularly Western creation, just as, later, the "right to air space" will be the element in which Air Force Marshall Goering dreams of installing *die fliegende nation*, the Nazi demos.[1] "Every German must learn to fly… Wings hang dormant under men's skins." Watching the launch of the first rockets, Hitler, who feels military defeat coming, tells Dornberger,

"If I had believed in your work, there would have been no need for war…"—*or at least there would have been no need for combat!*

To defeat, without fighting, a continental adversary who constantly exhausts himself by rushing into the spatial and temporal limits of the terrestrial battlefield is, as we know, what England will manage to do. Hitler, like Napoleon, will be defeated by the *fleet in being*,[2] which will constantly draw its victory from its inaccessibility to combat, from its abandonment of the harmful principle that we must attack as soon as the enemy is in sight, that we must shorten the distance between them and us. *The fleet in being is logistics taking strategy to its absolute point, as the art of movement of unseen bodies*; it is the permanent presence in the sea of an invisible fleet able to strike no matter where and no matter when, annihilating the enemy's will to power by creating a global zone of insecurity in which it will no longer be able to "decide" with certainty, to *want*—in other words, to win. Thus, it is above all a new idea of violence that no longer comes from direct confrontation and bloodshed, but rather from the unequal properties of bodies, evaluation of the number of movements allowed them in a chosen element, permanent verification of their dynamic efficiency. If Napoleon judged an army's strength in mechanical terms, Maurice de Saxe, one of the first on the European continent, understood that *violence can be reduced to nothing but movement*: "I am not in favor of battle," he states. "I am persuaded that an able general *can wage war his whole life long* without being *forced to do battle*." Nonetheless, in Western Europe, in a restricted and uneven terrain, one could not claim to "melt away the enemy" without eventually being driven to direct confrontation between ever larger military masses. German incarceration is the best example of this historical territorial constraint, which created the brief and bloody war-mongering of Prussian theory. On the immense nautical glacis, on the other hand, the home fleet could elude battle almost indefinitely; it was not forced by the adversary into *desperate combat* as long as it stayed out of reach, all the while remaining present.

Not to be driven to desperate combat, but to provoke a prolonged desperation in the enemy, to inflict permanent moral and material sufferings that diminish him and *melt him away*: this is the role of indirect strategy, which can make a population give up in despair without recourse to bloodshed. As the old saying goes, "Fear is the cruelest of assassins: it never kills, but keeps you from living." After all, the invention of happiness, that new idea in Europe according to Saint-Just, was perhaps no more for the continentals than a way of resisting the moral constraint come from the sea, the loss of their substance.

In 1914, it took the Allied blockade two years before the German civilians felt the initial effects, but these effects lasted well after the end of the terrestrial combat and were an indirect factor in Germany's subsequent economic failure. It was this prolonged despair that provided the ground for the hot-headed politics of Nazism, for the fascist domestication of the German people. In the same way, the rapid material and moral collapse that we are now seeing in Western Europe is the long-range result of the American geo-strategic turnaround, creating on our continent, from afar, a new economic and physiological crisis.

Favored by the merchant populations, indirect strategy reproduced in another element the effects of the old communal poliorcetics. Like the ancient "state of siege," it allowed one to "indefinitely prolong the hostilities" against the totality of populations that are no longer "civilian" but "continental." It represents the revival of capitalism because it is none other than the technical surpassing of the old fortified place, which was rendered obsolete and dismantled by the power of the new State armies. This is the answer to the exorbitant economic requirements of the continental military class, to its claim to dominate the flows of terrestrial traffic.

In the final account, economic liberalism is a perfect illustration of Errard de Bar-le-Duc's dictum: "The attack changed with the invention of machines to destroy." The bourgeoisie's sudden resistance to the concept of territorial warfare becomes from then on the guiding principle of a capitalism that, by becoming amphibious, applies total warfare on the sea and in the colonies; that jumps literally from "the great immobile machine" into the "mobile machine," making the oceans a "vast logistical camp"; that drags behind it a proletariat harnessed to the functioning of the naval vehicle, a proletariat of rowers who are the machine's true engine, its accelerator in time of battle.

Henceforth, it is no longer a question of crossing a continent or an ocean from one city to the next, one shore to the next. The fleet in being creates a new dromocratic idea: the notion of displacement without destination in space and time. It imposes the primordial idea of disappearance in distance, and no longer in the danger of cataclysm; it rushes non-stop toward the beyond. The end of the engine here becomes, necessarily and no matter how, the point of no return, the standard fate of the floating machine lost lock, stock and barrel, or simulating its own wreck, like those submarines that jettison fake debris and fuel to escape their pursuers, thus anticipating their actual disappearance; like those old warships hauled out to sea one last time to be sunk in the apotheosis of an ultimate explosion, the staging of great naval funerals where the vessel is sucked into the liquid funnel of the maelstrom—sucked in by its own rush toward the point of no return.

Gordon Pym and *Moby Dick* are only the anticipated narratives of the nuclear cruise. The strategic submarine has no need to go anywhere in particular; it is content, while controlling the sea, to remain invisible. But its hourly fate is already sealed. Furthermore, as soon as the fleet in being becomes a fundamental given of the Right to the Sea, the explorers, discoverers and raiders of every stripe, while continuing to seek uncharted lands, equally adhere to the invention of passages, in other words to the realization of the absolute, uninterrupted, circular voyage, since it involves neither departure nor arrival. The loop of no-return is traced in advance by the circular or triangular nautical routes of European mercantilism.

Thus a new category of political rights was created on the oceans: the "*right to the sea*," initially "an entity that was more emotional and poetic than rational," they said. It is true that the Mediterranean cities—overpopulated, insular nations poor in goods and surface area, dreaming of "working the sea" by creating a nautical demos—appear unwilling to be subjected to ancient terrestrial law. *The open sea* was to compensate for every social, religious and moral constraint, for every political and economic oppression, even for the physical laws due to the earth's gravity, to continental crampedness.

But the right to the sea very quickly became the right to crime, to a violence that was also freed from every constraint... Soon, the "empire of the seas" replaces the open sea. The seventeenth-century chronicler can see its fruits even from the shore, where reigns "the horrible industry of shipwreckers massacring and pillaging the survivors of shipwrecks that they provoke with their misleading fires..." On the high seas, he sees but "the excesses *sanctioned by the very practices of the sea...* The monstrous despotism that, in the name of commercial monopolies, aspires toward *exclusive domination* of the oceans...a kind of right to conquest exercised by the

Dutch, after Venice, Spain and Lisbon." And a little further on, he notes: "What is terrifying is that all these powerful nautical organizations were not the doings of States, but almost a spontaneous product of these nations' mercantile engineers, the State having played no further role other than to sanction them, to claim them for its own."

In the final account, it is not so surprising that a trafficker and buccaneer like Laffitte financed the publication of Marx's manifesto. His vision of the international State rising from society like "its product at a given moment in its evolution" rather closely resembles the spontaneous empire of the "sea rovers" from which comes the first industrial nation of the modern world. This totalitarian State is located everywhere and nowhere; it is obsessed by commercial exchanges; it serves only economic interests, and is bent on devouring and destroying its adversaries' goods. Its population has "broken loose from its moorings," left the earth; the first to conform absolutely to Marx's definition of the industrial proletariat: "Workers have no country…we must cut the umbilical cord that holds the worker to the earth."

In England, up until the nineteenth century, they recruit sailors by simply closing the ports under order of the king and rounding up the seamen. In seventeenth-century France, with the industrialization of naval warfare demanding an increasingly large personnel, they number and register the entire coastal population, declaring it "available and enrolled in a single, great army, serving by turns in war, in trade, and in land-development activities." This is called the class system. This first operation of State-instigated military proletarianization, which only barely precedes the French Revolution, is like the masses' first accession to public transport. There is also concern (rare for the time) about the new proletarian's "nationality."

Deported from total war, he must justify his origins; if he is a foreigner, he must be naturalized within five years. Desertion is severely punished and the State practices the social control of families by declaring itself the "protector of women and children," of conscripted workers.

Nonetheless, here again, the expansion of war was such that proletarianization found itself associated with judicial and police repression: they recruited by luck of the draw, and the proletariat saw itself mixed in with the troop of deportees and galley slaves that the courts "manufactured" in large number under governmental pressure.

In the seventeenth century, the naval proletariat is already, literally, a population of convicts, the "damned of the earth." Marx and Engels' new theoretical opposition to the followers of Proudhon is much like Colbert's reflection deploring French inability to create an all-powerful naval empire, their backwardness in the domain of colonization: "No companies, as long as we continue to imitate Marseilles... They would rather give up the best opportunity in the world than lose the pleasure of a country house. Moreover, they don't want great vessels, but only little boats, so that everyone will have his own..."[3] The creation of the *right to the sea*, as they conceive of it at the time, is ill compatible with the aptitude for terrestrial happiness, made of simplicity and independence, that is found in the South. In the same way, the social utopia will come less from class antagonism than from the hatred of the Earth, and we could make comparisons *ad infinitum* between the utopian project and the plans of the naval empire where Marx is buried.[4]

But it seems more interesting to consider the chronometric aspect of this empire that displaces its violence in the invisibility of the nautical glacis, a floating nation that resembles that other Time machine, History. In fact, victory (decision) in the world without reference point or accident of the fleet in being requires that one be situated, if nowhere on Earth, then at least in Time—in other words, in planetary mechanics. For this simple reason, the English will long remain the best clockmakers in the world. Mastery over the sea demands that over Time; it requires you to "shoot for the moon," as they used to say.

So it is natural that the modern formula of popular war will take shape—through English influence on islanders (Paoli in Corsica under Louis XV)—in a nation of navigators: Spain versus the French empire. In fact, popular war is already no longer *in* a given territory. Rather, it advocates the dispersal of the army corps within society itself (the new soldier will be "like a fish in water," and this allusion to the liquid element is hardly coincidental). Like the naval battle, popular war operates on the clash of dynamic bodies. It has to do with "the excesses sanctioned by the very practices of the sea," with absolute violence, with the disappearance of morals and preexisting laws. Popular war is total.

We have not paid enough attention, in Western History, to the moment when this transfer from the natural vitalism of the marine element (the ease with which one can lift, displace, glide weighty engines) to an inevitable technological vitalism[5] took place; the moment when the technical transport body left the sea like the unfinished living body of evolutionism, crawling out of its original environment and becoming amphibious. Speed as a pure idea without content comes from the sea like Venus, and when Marinetti cries that the universe has been enriched by a new beauty, the beauty of speed, and opposes the racecar to the Winged Victory of Samothrace, he forgets that he is really talking about the same esthetic: the esthetic of the transport engine. The coupling of the winged woman with the ancient war vessel and the coupling of Marinetti the fascist with his racecar, "ideal shaft crossing over the earth," whose wheel he controls, emerge from this technological evolutionism whose realization is more obvious than that of the living world. The right to the sea creates the right to the road of modern States, which through this become totalitarian States.

When Norman Angell states in *The Great Illusion* that war has become *economically futile* because it is no longer founded *on flight at the expense of the "exterior group,"* in other words on *portable wealth*, but rather, henceforth, on credit and the commercial contract, he is mistaken in thinking that this must radically suppress the "conqueror"; his discourse is somewhat lacking in rigor. In fact, what is revealed by this change in the nature of wealth is only a change in the speed of world economy, the passage from the movable unit to the hourly unit: *the war of Time*. With the fleet in being, England concentrates its efforts on technical innovation in the domain of transportation, and more precisely on the manufacture of rapid engines. It draws from this both its economic superiority and the orientation that made it the first great industrial nation, the model for all the others—engendering "that primordial feeling of technical superiority that gets confused with a feeling of general superiority." In fact, there was no "industrial revolution," but only a "dromocratic revolution;" there is no democracy, only dromocracy; there is no strategy, only dromology. It is precisely at the moment when Western technological evolutionism leaves the sea that the substance of wealth begins to crumble, that the ruin of the most powerful peoples and nations gets under way—*viz.* Carter's declarations about the end of the American dream. It is *speed* as the nature of dromological progress that ruins progress; it is the permanence of the war of Time that creates total peace, *the peace of exhaustion.*[6]

The SST affair, followed by that of the Concorde, illustrate this system of ruin (so ruinous that the advanced States must band together in order to maintain the production of these machines that are subject only to the law of speed). As at the origins of the fleet in being, the upkeep of the monopoly demands that every new engine be immediately superseded by a faster one. But the threshold of speed is constantly shrinking, and the faster engine is becoming more and more difficult to conceive of. It is often obsolete even before being used; the product is literally worn out before being operated, thus surpassing "by speed" the entire profit system of industrial obsolescence! When riches, accumulations and modes of production were freed from their enclosure, therefore, it was not to reach free enterprise, their socialization, but to reach *their own vehicular power*, their maximum dynamic efficiency. *This* is the "futility" of wealth that disappeared in the essence of dromological progress. Western man has appeared superior and dominant, despite inferior demographics, because he appeared *more rapid*. In colonial genocide or ethnocide, he was the survivor because he was in fact *super-quick (sur vif)*. The French word *vif*, "lively," incorporates at least three meanings: swiftness, speed (*vitesse*), likened to *violence*—sudden force, abrupt edge (*vive force, arête vive*), etc.—and to *life* (*vie*) itself: to be quick means to stay alive (*être vif, c'est être en vie*)!

With the realization of dromocratic type progress, humanity will stop being diverse. It will tend to divide only into *hopeful populations* (who are allowed the hope that they will reach, in the future, someday, the speed that they are accumulating, which will give them access to the possible—that is, to the project, the decision, the infinite: *speed is the hope of the West*) and *despairing populations*, blocked by the inferiority of their technological vehicles, living and subsisting in a finite world.

Thus, the related logic of knowing-power, or power-knowledge, is eliminated to the benefit of moving-power—in other words the study of tendencies, of flows. This is so obvious that, in the last five years, they have stopped teaching geography in the French Military Academy and the police have started experimenting with the "criminostat."[7]

Empires with colossal territories such as China, despite their attempts at "modernization," have had to submit to this pure, new order without content since the nineteenth century, finding nothing to oppose the penetration with. And today, the Chinese and Vietnamese people's armies are undergoing a difficult revision, by splitting themselves into a technical (rapid) army and an army of the people, represented as "animal value" (slow), and therefore, more specifically, "survival value" in the event of a nuclear holocaust. As to the latter, we could recall that in 1932 the Chinese population of Shanghai had already played this role: it was, in fact, among the first in the world to suffer Japanese experiments with massive air attacks aiming at the total destruction of urban centers. The German military command had also scrutinized the social fallout when elaborating their own "security plans": false alarms, exercises, system of urban shelters, etc., which in the mind of the political leaders must have contributed largely to the psychological formation of the German citizenry. By a curious twist of fate, it is now the Chinese who have been greatly inspired by this national socialistic mobilization...

In the war of Time, the social "beyond" of populations has become the "beyond" of the zero-hour, as the revolutionary's last hope.

To extract a purely technological, military element from a population in arms was thus a capital political decision for the Chinese leaders, for nowhere else had armies and populations remained so biologically associated, up to and including in the tools they used. This revolutionary unity is brutally destroyed by the discovery of other evidence. The class struggle is replaced by the struggle of the *technological bodies of the armies according to their dynamic efficiency:* air force versus navy, ground army versus police/politics, etc. A caricature of this situation has existed in Latin America for some time now.

2

Practical War

Hoorah! No more contact
with the vile earth!
— Marinetti, 1905

IN 1914, the military high command in Europe was still following Clausewitz or Napoleon. It concentrated on exerting its will in a ground war of rapid penetration, of short and decisive battles. The advantage of this type of conflict was that it skirted around the problems posed by the military distribution of territories, since the logistical effort required would be of little importance, and especially of little constancy—a war, in a sense, with no terrain, or at best having little to do with it!

We are still in the mentality of the Vienna Congress; the European monarchic powers that feel the end coming give a final sign of life. Like Clausewitz in *Vom Kriege*, they try desperately to draw a line between absolute and total war. Total war is omnipresent; it is first waged on the sea because the naval glacis naturally presents no permanent obstacle to a vehicular movement of planetary dimensions. Nonetheless, this type of totalitarian conflict can be realized on the earth only on condition of setting up infra structures that are durable in ubiquity. As Vauban remarks, we should be able to superimpose war onto all the inhabitable parts of the universe.

"Ubique quo fas et gloria ducunt": the English engineers ended up significantly reducing their motto to UBIQUE… "everywhere." This means the universe redistributed by the military engineers, the earth "communicating" like a single glacis, as the infra structure of a future battlefield.[1] This is the world that is transformed "from a landscape as workshop into a planned landscape, an imperial space," as Lukács remarks about German socialism. When Renan welcomed Lesseps into the French Academy, he reproached him "for having sought peace and found war" by making the Suez Canal a new Bosphorus. A century has passed without contradicting Renan's prophecy; the penetration of the Suez isthmus is an old polytechnician's dream for which a number of Saint Simonian engineers died. Its realization was then considered by the military experts a new index of reliability in the totality of international communications, a considerable acceleration point on the network of inferences of worldwide strategy. By "redesigning the map of the world," they opened the way to the "transport of war" toward the East, as well as to the new vertical trusts. With the great geo-strategic revolution of the nineteenth century, social and economic organization begins to depend entirely on that of the space of activity as the place of transference, and the phenomenon of war begins to feed itself by creating the sources of its own conflicts and multiplying them: they are still dying for Suez or Panama.

In 1914, however, rural, enclosed France was still scarcely favorable to the development of the military transport's omnipresence; the conflict carried by its heavy mobile engines lost no time in sinking with them. War stopped being a brief, charming promenade, a touristic stroll. The adversaries bury each other and come to know battles without precedent, since they can last, as at Verdun, for an entire year—from February to December, 1916. *Armies could no longer simply come and go.*

At this point, the French reaction is significant. They first want to maintain political distance, and they still come back to the communal schema as a guarantee of internal order. The country is cut in two by a demarcation line: a "civilian" France, the rear guard, with its democratic government, its economic and industrial activities, its new matriarchy of female suppliers (who will give the feminist struggle its dubious nature); and a "military" France, the army zones, fortified glacis where, Ferry notes: "The supreme commander is no longer a chief of war, *but the administrator of a territory*"[2]—a territory in which civilian power hoped to crystallize the battle and enclose its military proletariat in an absolute war, a war "without limitations in the use of violence," but one that would not spread, could not be brought into the interior.

This is the war of attrition. For the high command, the enormous wear on the troops and material, the modern form of decimation, was still, at the beginning of the war, a gold star in a general's career! It was considered a mark of the military commander's great activity, of his personality, even of the orthodoxy of his art, in the jargon of the schools of war—"absence of goodheartedness," "unlimited use of force," which allow one, according to Clausewitz, not to retreat in the face of bloodshed. But here again, the Prussian general found himself rapidly outmoded, he who thought, along with many of his contemporaries, that the social situation of civilized States would finally render their wars much less cruel and destructive than those of other nations.

Only several months after the beginning of the hostilities, Ferry shows us how difficult it is—since one of the newest jobs for the personnel assigned the logistical task is the *rational evaluation of the army's obsolescence*—to calculate the damage inflicted by the new industrial war fast enough to compensate in time for the pure and simple disappearance of the two parties on the battlefield, something that had never been seen before. The voluntary war of attrition was both the first war of disappearance and the first of consumption: disappearance of men, material, cities, landscapes; and unbridled consumption of munitions, material, manpower.

Little by little, the elegant battle plans and orders of attack give way to new considerations: consumption of grenades by trench yard, production programs, balance and evaluation of supplies—during an attack in 1917, for example, they consume 6,947,000 explosive shells on the French side, or 28% of the existing stock... But they also speak in terms of "daily consumption of artillery." The theory of the high command disappears in what is henceforth called "practical war"—that which makes war convenient, *easier to use*; that which keeps it from getting bogged down in its own impossiblities. The French Ministries of War and that of Weapons are separated, the latter headed by the famous Loucheur, who prefigures Bush and Speer, the technocrats of total war.

The war of attrition marks a new threshold: bourgeois society had believed it could enclose absolute violence in the ghetto of the army zone but, deprived of space, war had spread into human Time—the war of attrition was also the war of Time. Like the troops of Year II, the mobile mass of 1914 had been thrown into battle with a cry of "*ultreia*!" But the battle was finally reduced to a series of individual actions, a war of petty officers, a succession of brief runs toward death succeeding each other day by day, from month to month, at the same place; or else of "long vacations" for the immobile men, waiting for the end where they lay, nailed to the ground by the power of the bombardments. Proletarian lodging in the "army zones" replaces the swamp of the "urban zone." The no man's land has become a suburb, a neutralizing space in which the promise of movement is no longer accomplished, and the loss of movement for the national fortress is first the *loss of good health*, then death. Revolts and mutinies on the part of soldiers refusing the assault succeed the disorder of the urban riot, the stationing of the masses in the city, before becoming in the debacle "simple civil war," as Engels had predicted to Lassalle—a rerouting toward the interior of the "proletariat's torrent of energy" (Trotsky). In 1917 in France national war lost its old revolutionary prestige in the eyes of the masses, simply because it was no longer able to "advance." It no longer reached the Assault's superior speed, no longer won the race against death, against the engine of war.

The voyage of the masses once more took them from the street to the rail road, the street in which they paraded while singing and counting off steps before a city population applauding the departure of the fearsome armed mob. After that, the military livestock quickly jumped on the cattle wagon, but everything was over very fast. As Captain de Poix notes, "So many times had I seen our infantry leave for battle, magnificent in their enthusiasm, only to be suddenly cut down by an unsuspected machine gun; in the space of several minutes the battlefield was littered with corpses."

The good captain thus had the stroke of genius to remedy the troops' *stasis*. He conceived of "armored cars going over all kinds of terrain," and, from November 25, 1915, he promoted the large scale manufacture of this new kind of war machine. By January 31, 1916, they built 400 assault tanks, and as soon as they appeared on the battlefield their psychological effect was tremendous. The generals were soon screaming by the millions for those "automotive forts," the new technical object that so perfectly realized a strategic philosophy obsessed by Frederick the Great's dictum: "To win is to advance!" Soon Ferry could write, before he himself was cut down in the attack of Vauxaillon, "French morale has reached an unprecedented degree of exaltation. Last month, the soldiers on leave from Parnay found their leave too long, *and they returned to the front as if they were going on vacation*... They already saw themselves at the Meuse or the Rhine! *I unleash my every dream*..."

Speed is the hope of the West; it is speed that supports the armies' morale. What "makes war convenient" is transportation, and the armored car, able to go over every kind of terrain, erases the obstacles. With it, earth no longer exists. Rather than calling it an "all terrain" vehicle, they should call it "*sans terrain*"—it climbs embankments, runs over trees, paddles through the mud, rips out shrubs and pieces of wall on its way, breaks down doors. It escapes the old linear trajectory of the road or the railway. It offers a whole new geometry to speed, to violence. It is already no longer simply an auto-mobile, but also a projectile and launcher, while waiting to become a radio transmitter as well; it hurls both projectiles and itself. With it, once more, Death kills Death, since it victoriously opposes the fearsome German machine gun. Captain de Poix has a prophetic vision of a battlefield literally covered by the mass of these automotive forts. After leaving the street, the military proletariat loses contact with the road. From now on, anything can become a probable trajectory of its Assault. The battlefield has become like the naval glacis, without obstacles, entirely run by the rapid engines, the "battleships of the earth."

The war of attrition had, from lack of space, spread out into Time; duration was survival. All-terrain (or rather, sans-terrain) assault extends war over an earth that disappears, crushed under the infinity of possible trajectories. We suddenly find ourselves facing a new "right to the earth." Just as totalitarian as the right to the sea, it implies for the masses another phenomenology of becoming. The rush of Assault-mobiles prolongs the mad rush of auto-taxis leaving the Parisian pavement in 1914 and heading for the Marne, "the last romantic battle, in which the archaic part of the war came to an end" (Jean de Pierrefeu). The speed of military transport is no longer only "a metaphor for a vertiginous passage of existential time." The speedometer of the assault engine is literally, for its passengers, an "existential quantifier," a measure of sur-vival!

It is interesting to note the attitude of the British high command at this capital juncture in dromological progress: from the first continental assaults, this nautical people once more takes to the open sea, unconcerned about enclosing itself in an infrangible continental battle. "He prefers the war of machines"—they should say engines—"to the war of chest beating," goes a popular saying. They have 500,000 men on the sea and 3,000,000 in the arsenals and factories. If they participate with an obvious ill will in the hodge-podge of command, it is nonetheless understandable that they are the first to want to launch on the terrestrial battlefield, to the north of the Somme, the "battleships of the earth"—sans-terrain assault engines for which they will have a lasting affection, as we saw in the desert in 1942…

Part 3

DROMOCRATIC SOCIETY

1

Unable Bodies

Risk—but in comfort!

— Marshal Goering

HERMAN GOERING BECAME a pilot in the First World War because he had a tendency toward rheumatism and thus, as a foot soldier, suffered from the long marches.

In the course of the various battles, especially since the seventeenth century, awareness had grown of the increasing problem of military infirmity. A flourishing industry developed: orthopedics. It was discovered that the damage caused by the war machines to the mechanics of the surviving bodies could be compensated for by other machines—prostheses. While in France the handicapped are exempt from military service, this is not the case in Germany: in 1914, the German army had few or no exemptions, for it had decided to *make physical handicaps functional* by using each man according to his specific disability: the deaf will serve in heavy artillery, hunchbacks in the automobile corps, etc. Paradoxically, the dictatorship of movement exerted on the masses by the military powers led to the promotion of unable bodies. The use of the technical vehicle is at this point so assimilated to that of the surgical prosthesis that it will be some time before the French military command finally hands the tanks over to personnel other than the "one quarter sick with malaria, the rest rehabilitated young men who had never seen battle" (Renaudel's report).

In 1921, Marinetti metaphorizes about the armored car: the overman is over-grafted, an *inhuman type* reduced to a driving—and thus deciding—principle, an animal body that disappears in the superpower of a metallic body able to annihilate time and space through its dynamic performances. Vain attempts have been made to fit Marinetti's works into various artistic and political categories; but Futurism in fact comes from a single art—that of war and its essence, speed. Futurism provides the most accomplished vision of the dromological evolutionism of the 1920s, the measure of super-speed! In fact, the human body huddling in the "steel alcove" is not that of the bellicose dandy seeking the rare sensations of war, but of the doubly-unable body of the proletarian soldier. Deprived, as he has always been, of will, he now requires physical assistance from a vehicular prosthesis in order to accomplish his historical mission, Assault. The dromomaniac's kinetic superpower is suddenly devalued. The war of attrition had already shown the disdain in which a mobile mass reduced to inaction was held, and the nature of the treatment reserved for it. Practical war revealed its impotence as a dominant dromocratic agent, the motor and producer of speed on the continent. Nonetheless, the world war having sanctioned the high command's intellectual bankruptcy and the triumph of industrial warfare, everyone felt an insatiable need for manpower. The processes of military proletarianization proved more than ever to be indissociable from those of industrial proletarianization for the generals who, despite themselves, had become "territorial administrators."

Ferry states: "*Now everyone knows that the structure of a battlefield exists*... The greatest possible technical distribution of terrain is necessary, and if it takes 200,000 men to bring it about, then the government will negotiate with its allies." "Countries such as Italy and Portugal have admirable reserves of men...Here you would not even notice the shortages imposed by the war," writes an official emissary in 1916. Governments bargain over and hastily exchange their working-class cattle, bragging about "their resistance to low temperatures, their sobriety and their aptitude for labor." They dip heavily into colonial properties, Creoles or Blacks from Senegal, workers from Morocco, and especially tireless navies from Indochina by the tens of thousands—other natives such as the Madagascans preferably being reserved for combat... If naval warfare, by becoming permanent and total, engendered one of the first mass mobilizations, the perspective of total warfare on the continent, as early as in 1914, obviously requires a new social project, an original type of proletarianization.

Practical war divides the Assault into two phases, the first of which is the creation of the original infrastructure of future battlefields. This infrastructure consists of new railroads and stations, telephone installations, enlargement of roads and tracks, the parallel lines of departure, evacuation routes, shelters, etc. The countryside, the earth is henceforth given over, definitively consecrated to war by the cosmopolitan mass of workers, an army of laborers speaking every language, the Babel of logistics.[1] Both the arsenal and the war personnel already take on a kind of peaceful, or rather political, air; they return to highway surveillance. Already we find the beginnings of what will become deterrence: reduction of power in favor of a better trajectory, life traded for survival. The status quo is the depletion of the earth. In 1924, the military monk Teilhard de Chardin writes in *Mon univers*: "We still need mightier and mightier cannons, bigger and bigger battleships, to materialize *our aggression on the world.*"

Dromocratic intelligence is not exercised against a more or less determined military adversary, but as a permanent assault on the world, and through it, on human nature. The disappearance of flora and fauna and the abrogation of natural economies are but the slow preparation for more brutal destructions. They are part of a greater economy, that of the blockade, of the siege; strategies, in other words, of depletion.

The economic war currently ravaging the earth is but the *slow phase* of declared war, of a rapid and brief assault to come, for this is what perpetuates, in non-combat, military power as class power. From time immemorial, the caste of hunter-raiders has been unproductive, although it provided the group's food. Along with the science of weapons, it has always fostered methods of depletion—what today we call *food power*. Thus when Venice, that floating nation, that country in which no one had ever "set foot," stopped being the premier economic and naval power because of the discovery of America and the new Atlantic politics of Europe, it providently turned back to the interior, to agrarian power and terrestrial property, for it knew that the loss of *sea power* meant an immediate threat of suffering *food power*, always the law of the two types of humanity.

In the same way, the United States, after their first failure at intensive conquest in the 1930s ("declare peace in the world"), today lead a war without mercy against Green Europe (campaign against the peasants, control of food industries, grain embargoes, etc.). It is precisely the "futility of wealth" that provides the ground for conquest. American dollar-politics is only one sign of the *intensive growth* of American military might, momentarily robbed of its *extensive growth* by the failure in Vietnam and the nuclear standoff. But here again we must admire the speed with which the U.S. replaced their geo-strategic bombardments on North Vietnam (systematic destruction of flora and fauna in the rural environment) with an impressive abandonment of technological material when they retreated from the terrain, making their enemies their best customers, as General Giap's recent declarations could lead us to believe.[2]

Timeless dromological methods: in the seventeenth-century, when Colbert launches his economic politics with the idea of promoting "national wealth," a "national product," he prepares the way for Louvois' war-effort by "making sure needs are created," by triggering in his neighbors "the prodigious consumption of his so numerous products," as Sir William Temple says.

For his war-sites, Louvois was directly inspired by Roman proletarianization, while Colbert reproduced the Athenian economic system that had finally brought about the collapse of Lacedaemonian power. As Lyautey writes in 1901, "The tactic of economic penetration alone is worth every other taught in the military academy." The dromocratic expansion of Greece had also found itself blocked at every turn by the military status quo. The native barbarians had learned to organize militarily in the West. The other colonial satellites collaborated in Greek politics. It is at this point that Athens renounced its system of extensive (rapid) penetration to adopt a system of intensive (slow) penetration; external military engagements were replaced by the abrogation of natural economies in the interior (agrarian reform, urbanization, creation of workshops and factories, etc.).

Athenian currency, spread over the entire Mediterranean basin, pouncing on the economies of the big cities, created such an inflation of exchanges that it became fatal—notably to Sparta's equilibrium, which for its part had chosen the opposite solution:

conservation of the State apparatus by abolishing military and monetary movement.[3]

Aristotle wrote the epitaph to Lycurgus' system: "The essential object of any social system must be to organize the military institution *like all the others.*"

In Sparta the opposite happened. In the first Hellenic democracy we already find most of the great Western themes, except for the main one: mobility. Whereas everything was sacrificed to make the State a single war machine, the eventuality of its being mobilized in a real conflict seemed fearsome to the Lacedaemonians, as if the hazards and uncertainties of battle would destroy their overly precise military mechanism.[4]

The Spartans have been called a people without history. In reality, by their hostility to every form of constitutional metamorphosis, they *refused* History as the kinetic reference of their existence. First, by not turning toward the sea and its vehicular empires—thus separating themselves from the totality of Hellenic cities—to go settle in the very heart of Greece and colonize the Messenians, Greeks like themselves. Then, by eluding for almost two centuries after the Lycurgean experiment the consequences of their military might, by fleeing those of their victories. And it will be precisely the Spartan military State's victory over Athens that will subvert its perfection: "The Lacedaemonians might date the beginning of their corruption from their conquest of Athens, and the influx of gold and silver among them that thence ensued" (Plutarch, "Life of Agis").

What the armies couldn't do was accomplished by economic warfare. The dilemma of the status quo, of military non-intervention, was resolved once and for all, not only for the Mediterraneans, but for the Western world to come.

By the middle of the third century, following the collapse of the Lycurgean immobile machine, there remained only about a hundred Spartans who still owned shares of the State. The rest of the population, says Plutarch, became a miserable crowd without legal status, a social mass that the military State had taught to live only for a war that would never come, and that from now on didn't know what to do with its existence. When the State itself survived as no more than a dream of the past, a handful of remaining sadistic customs, the Spartan world sank entirely into anomie.

The West persists in repeating Plutarch's lesson, "obeying a law that it doesn't even know, but that it could recite in its sleep." *Stasis is death* really seems to it to be *the general law of the World.* The dromocrat constantly stifles the democrat of Lycurgus'—and Mao's—original revolution. It is enough to hear the speeches of today's Chinese leaders about "consumer goods" to know that the old thinker did no more than delay the institution in China of the West's fearsome system of intensive growth, and whether it is conveyed by orthodox Marxism or liberalism is of little import! Just as Hitler could only begin lightning warfare through the economic system of Doctor Schacht, and Roosevelt could only begin total warfare through the New Deal.

Stasis is death, the general law of the world. The State-fortress, its power, its laws exist in places of intense circulation. In a recent work, Georges Huppert attacks the common notion that the *general and positive sense* of history appeared in the eighteenth century and gave rise to important works only in the nineteenth.[5] He cites the example of a group of erudites, *mostly of the legal profession,* who, toward the middle of the sixteenth century, proposed (in the words of one of them, La Popeliniere) "an idea of perfect history." At the same time, the new European States were tending among themselves to reestablish the notion of legitimate war (or legalistic war), in the Roman manner (Livy, I, 32, 5–15). The State's historical ideality comes out as soon as war itself is reborn in ideal forms, is technically distinguished (thanks to centralism) from a simple punitive expedition, and tears itself loose from local compromises to approach a rigorous original concept.

In fact, history progresses at the speed of its weapons systems. At the end of the fifteenth century, it is still for Commynes a stable memory, a model to be reproduced. Annals are seasonal, like the war that returns every year in springtime. Linear time is eliminated, as it was from the ancient fortress in which "the enemy Time" was beaten by the static resistance of the construction materials—by duration.

Historical creation also begins to function like the ancient war machines that carried out their destructive movements on the spot even after the invention of the ballista and the catapult (around 405, at the siege of Motza). If Hegel "gets bored seeing Livy repeat for the hundredth time descriptions of battles against the Volscians, occasionally limiting his narrative to: 'In this year, war was successfully waged against the Volscians,'" complaining of the "abstract representations," it is because the historical content is literally that of a communique (the first ephemeris of projected societies, comparable to what, in the nineteenth century, the monotonous detail of secret police reports represents for a sociology that becomes more widespread). Here we are dealing with works that are practical in ways that Hegel could not imagine.

And if Livy endlessly resumes the litany of his commentary, it is because repetition is then the means of reaching vaster fields, a work-in-progress.[6] The narrative material can only function by being repeated one hundred times. Through repetition, it eliminates chance and makes the Reason in these stories a war machine that deploys its forces by multiplying them. In the same way, it is understandable that just when artillery and military highway surveillance became part of the State system, especially under Sully, historical language passed literally from the *comparative* to the *positive*; in other words, *with no comparison of intensity!*

Accession to history becomes accession to movement, distant result of the accession to power of those "border prowlers, idlers of Apocalypse, living free of material cares at the edge of their domesticated abyss" (Julien Gracq), populations that appear and disappear on the borders of the Roman Empire, "thumbing their noses at war," on whom, as Livy adds, *"it clearly cannot be imposed."*

In the beginning of our era, the wave of dromocratic elites comes from Germany, from the banks of the Danube or elsewhere, and finally breaks over Western Europe. Suddenly, it is no longer might that makes right, but invasion, the power-to-invade. The hierarchy of the raid, born on the road during the "unbridled exodus of the mob of hunter-raiders, is superseded by the protocol of the stopover and of apportionment." When finally this dromocratic power abusively settles on the European territory, it still doesn't change the nature of its constitutional schema and, in guise of being dispersed, the organization of feudal society will remain that of troops on the march.

"The relations between the various lords were exactly defined, and despite haggling and petty bickering, when an important war or a crusade regrouped this ever-armed milieu, every knight knew exactly where his place was." The hierarchic distribution is already a marching order, the layout of territory a theater of operations. The architecture of command posts plays the same part as that of the pelagic acropolis or of the Algerian blockhouse. The feudal role is semi-colonial, since it perfectly distinguishes *the mastery over the earth* by the military occupier from its *landed ownership* by the native.

"*For the dromocratic State, mastery over the earth is already the mastery over its dimensions.*"

The ancient cadastral law prolonged nothing else, as Colonel Barrader writes in *Fossatum Africae*: "Centuriation is the very foundation of mass education, of their civilization…the indelible trace of a possession-taking that *divides to conquer*." This indelible dichotomy is the one that exists between the nature of the moving-power of invasion and that of the landowner's (or sedentary worker-producer's) relative inability to move, to displace himself, attached as he is to his little parcel of land; the dichotomy between the geography of the inhabitant and that of the passer-by. The *trace* of the Roman path is usually no more than a continuous line, held over from the general schema of centuriation. Thus everything is simple: the military State is on the road, the payment of the cadastral tax is evaluated by the meter coverable, and thus defendable, we could say, by the army, the troop of horsemen, "that luxury-people."

The semi-colonial function has always been a protection racket in which the productive mass' safety is guaranteed by the tribute, remuneration for effective technological surveillance of the territory. In the same way, the Carolingian administration will be one that "straddles" for the benefit of a dromocratic State, which is careful not to demolish its internal constitution by founding hereditary land laws, or even by enlarging the royal domains (except for those that lie along the great vectors—the Meuse, for example—where its morphology "naturally" resides) in an attempt to lay its hands on all media, religious ideologies, money, knowledge, external commerce, modes of transportation and information, etc.

The Carolingian Capitularies advise the "masters of the earth" living in the ancient Roman villas (gradually transformed into command posts) to limit their land-clearing and to set up an alliance between the small and middle-sized native landowners by granting them if need be a certain on-the-spot military defense. Domination of the territorial ensemble by the occupant of the donjon (from the Latin *dominus*, "lord") is nonetheless tempered by the modest material means of what is still no more than a dispersed and foreign military minority, limited in their control of space and society, in the contributions they can exact from the native social corpus. It was also for security reasons that the Frank nobility had preferred the transparency of a populated countryside (soon overpopulated by essentially independent workers, occupied first with clearing the vast expanse of the land, then with maintaining the surrounding environment) to the impenetrable complexity of the original city.

But beyond this, *the transparency of the clearing* means maintenance of the invader's specific right over a territory in which he claims to settle, of his power to penetrate. The erection of the hillock, then of the donjon, is another answer to the problem of mastery over dimension, the latter becoming perspective, geometry of the gaze from an omnipresent fixed point—and no longer, as it was before, from the synoptic route of the horseman.

At this point, it is significant to see the cultivation of the earth restricted to an intensive exploitation of the cleared parcels, instead of spreading to the nearby wilderness through a new forward leap of the pioneering adventure.[7] The *phenomenon of retention* has been explained by an insufficiency of agricultural technology. But I think that we must look beyond the obvious material necessities—hunting, picking, gathering of building lumber in a nearby forest, etc.—to imperious strategic necessities created by the *technological insufficiencies of the military protector*, rather than by those of the gardener or the settler to whom the lord owed assistance and comfort in time of alarm.

Recent accounts have shown the relation between the limits of the clearing and that of human vision from an elevated site. The pioneer is more clearly called a *pathfinder* by the Anglo-Saxons. Land-clearing, the cultivation of the earth for subsistence, the receding of forest darkness, are in reality the creation of a military glacis as field of vision, of one of those frontier deserts spoken of by Julius Caesar, which, he says, represent the glory of the Empire because they are like a permanent invasion of the land by the dromocrat's look and, beyond this, because the speed of this vision—ideally without obstacles—causes *distances to approach.* A well-known photographer writes in his memoirs that his first darkroom was his childhood bedroom, that his first lens was a luminous slit in the closed shades. In this sense, the original donjon plays the part of Marey's chrono-photography; the military lookout-post offers the invader a constant view of the social environment, primary information. Social privilege is based on the choice of viewpoint (before attaching itself to accidents of fortune or birth), on the relative position that one manages to occupy, then organize, in a space dominating the trajectories of movement, keys to communication, river, sea, road, or bridge. Whence the extraordinary diversity of social treatments in the Middle Ages, a diversity that simply represents the variety of geographical views over a "realm" that, until the nineteenth century, doesn't appear in the texts as a formal territorial entity. The hereditary right reluctantly granted in 877 by Charles the Bald (Kiersy Capitulary) will transform possession of the dominant place into permanent social domination. A famous example is that of the Grimaldis in Monaco. The promontory overlooking the sea has since Prehistory been a privileged place; it will change hands several times throughout Antiquity before landing, by ruse, in the hands of the Grimaldis. From the tenth century onward, this family will not stop extracting honors and privileges from that initial appropriation of a dominant viewpoint. If we can then speak of class societies, we can only do so by designating the classes according to place, as we suggested earlier. If class struggles develop, they happen openly on the terrain, for the conquest of a dominant place. When the citadel or fortress is besieged, it is not simply a military, or even political, event, but a social one. Serious conflicts erupt, for example, when the protecting mission, the limit of the military scam, is violated by the feudal lords; when the "masters of the earth" claim to become its owners. In other words, when they try to unite in their hands alone the twin schemas of spatial appropriation of territory, robbing the native populations by trying to reduce their descendants to the level of *servi casati,* to the fate of tenant slaves—manpower deprived of its right to military defense.

2

The Boarding of Metabolic Vehicles[1]

Yours is not to reason why!

— Frederick the Second to his soldiers

THE EXTENSIVE PHASE of Assault requires quick deaths; the intensive preparatory phase inflicts slow ones. As Lieutenant-General von Metsch writes in *Wie wurde ein neuer krieg aussehen?* in the 1930s, "In total war, everything is a front! But along with the new total front, we would be wise to include *the nation's spiritual front*...In both the practical matter of preparation for rearmament and theoretical military discussions, the moral question is of primary importance."

Born of the sea, total war, according to Admiral Friedrich Ruge, aims "at destroying the honor, the identity, the very soul of the enemy." By striking populations with slow death through the destruction of their environment, the ultimate forms of modern ecological war curiously restore the "soul" in its primitive, "ethnological" definitions: "mana," potential substance indistinguishable from its environment, not individual but plural, multiform, fluidiform, coagulated here and there in social, animal or territorial bodies.

Dromological progress, by imposing the idea of two types of body, dependent on their situation in space, also imposes the idea of two types of soul: one weak, indecisive and vulnerable because it is dependent on its environment; the other powerful because it has put its "mana," its will, out of reach thanks to its deterritorialization, to the sophistication of its economy and viewpoint.

Clausewitz says nothing else when he answers the question, "What is war?" with, "War is an act of force to compel our enemy to do our will." We cannot exclude from war the problem of wills, despite the fact that Clausewitz immediately mutilates and bastardizes his definition by hastening to add that there can be no moral violence outside of the concepts of State and law. In fact, more than political and intelligent objectives of warfare, more than social or national rivalries, Clausewitz's definition already suggests *the creation of the "presence in the world" of bodies without will.* More than of an art of war, we think here of "techniques of animal bodies," an indelible dichotomy between the invader's moving-power and his relative inability to free his movements from the herd of workers.

Depending on the time and the latitude, the multitude of bodies with no soul, living dead, zombies, possessed, etc., is imposed all throughout history: a slow-motion destruction of the opponent, the adversary, the prisoner, the slave; an economy of military violence likening the human cattle to the ancient stolen herd of the hunter-raiders, and by extension, in modernized and militarized European societies, to the soulless bodies of children, women, men of color and proletarians.

In total war, the Nazis will do nothing different when they create an internal social front against the foreign bodies of Jews, gypsies and Slays. The deportation camps are but the laboratories in which the cattle are treated industrially—put to work in the mines, on logistical worksites, subjected to medical or social experiments, the ultimate recuperation of fats, bones, hair… Or, a happier final solution, as exchange value for other energy sources: fuel, trucks and military vehicles, through the intermediary of neutral countries; a whole classical economy of hostages, abductions and displacements—the preferred forms of dromocratic violence.

The precious lesson of the camps and the gulags has not been heeded, because it was erroneously presented not only as an ideological phenomenon, but also as a static one, an enclosure. Its absolute "inhumanity" was but the ostensible reintroduction in history of the original social bestiary, of the immense mass of domestic bodies, bodies unknown and unknowable. What else has the proletariat been since antiquity, if not an entirely domesticated category of bodies, a prolific, engine-towing class, the phantom presence in the historical narrative of a floating population linked to the satisfaction of logistical demands?

In the various descriptions of Western Europe in the ninth century, they sometimes mention the existence of certain *forenses*, who never constitute less than 16 percent of the recorded population. These are the migrant workers, going from one populated area to another without being granted their land-clearing occupation, except in Germany and perhaps in Champagne.

This social surplus, so similar to the "fourth world" of contemporary urban ghettos, comes directly from the phenomenon of strategic retention mentioned above; from feudal, then communal, social control.

In fact, the fortress's organic function could only be maintained by setting its limits, as well as those of the size of populations and the areas of extension. Strategic calculation is likened to statistical calculation. The fortress, with its entrances and exits, is a primary schema of the strategic calculator. The settling of armed society in the Middle Ages thus implied the disappearance of a habitat that until then had been considered common: *the disappearance of civilian space*, of the common man's right to space, to its qualification.

From this point on, we can no longer speak of a "class society" without questioning the poliorcetic schema of medieval society. This return to the old *dike*, this selective Reason, replaces civil rights with political rights, as in the Aristotelian reflection: "Aristocrats seek the plurality of fortified positions, oligarchic regimes prefer acropoles, and democrats like flat spaces." Since politics is a matter of terrain, we then see a veritable carving of human time and space that puts an end to the nation of *civil peace*.

Social conflicts arise from rivalries between those who occupy and preserve an eco-system as the place that specifies them as a family or group, and that therefore deserves every sacrifice, including sudden death. For if "to be is to inhabit" (in ancient German, *buan*), not to inhabit is no longer to exist. Sudden death is preferable to the slow death of he who is no longer welcome, of the reject, of the man deprived of a specific place *and thus of his identity.*

In short, the fortresses of the Middle Ages replaced primitive welcomes and sacred ancient hospitality with permanent social rejection as the primary necessity for the workings of the war machine. For this enclosed society, legal repression can only be a constraint to departure, to exodus, in other words, to deterritorialization as a loss of identity.

Surplus populations disappear in the obligatory movement of the voyage. The increasingly numerous bodies rejected by the poliorcetic order become physical forces moving nowhere, unseen zones, the immeasurable interstices of the strategic schema, the tolerated movement of perilous pilgrimages, of children's crusades, of the poor ("vagabonds without work, every able-bodied mendicant").

They are forbidden to remain for more than twenty-four hours within the communal fortress, and are driven out of other cities; the citizens themselves are forbidden to shelter them under pain of stiff fines. The Hundred Years' War will put an end to these great migrations. Already artillery was revolutionizing the battlefield.

But from the twelfth century onward, the influence of monetary media had grown considerably, announcing the end of the medieval status quo, that highly praised equilibrium of political and military organizations. The traditional *ost*-system is accompanied by remunerations. Knights soon receive wages. For a time, the military personnel is chosen primarily from among the gentry—the youngest son, for example, serving as a *private servant* and receiving a sizable salary—until the necessities of recruitment finally render the origins of the mercenaries rather dubious. Highwaymen and swashbucklers, descendants of Plautus' anti-heroes, "enemies common to all humanity," as Isocrates called them—these itinerant market objects are like the rest of the peasantry. Since antiquity, their condition has been scarcely better than that of the slave, who, at least, might be freed in wartime and drafted into the armed forces, especially the Navy, which required a large number of coordinated mechanical maneuvers, while land warfare was still considered a thing of "free men."

The military proletariat finds itself mixed in with the permanent exodus of the mobile masses; it issues from them as did the migrant worker of the nineteenth century or the illegal alien of the twentieth. The highwayman circulates; as his name suggests, he roams the highway. *This is his class space* as he travels in search of uncertain, seasonal employment. Callot will later depict him as a "capitano de baroni," a ragged and mutilated braggart, a fearsome, pitiful vagabond still sporting plume and banner in the interminable procession of the *miseries of war.*

The problem of temporary lodging for these warlike "gyrovagues" was posed like that of passing residence at the hospice or the lazaretto. Military monasticism will answer this problem, just as regular monasticism had answered the fixity of the mystical Gyrovagues, by instituting enclosures. The State will then intervene, substituting revenue systems for public charity and local duties such as the "franc sale" (the right to buy and sell salt tax-free), before the profitability of the social excess as work force becomes the most obvious solution: obligatory labor only slightly foreshadows obligatory military service, at least in France. A very peculiar obligation, since it must never hinder the prerogatives of independent manufacturers. Factory work must not escape the dictatorship of movement. It reproduces the enclosure on the spot, in an obligatory and absurd kinetic cycle, the slow death of the reject. I remember staying, about thirty years ago, on the banks of the Loire river near a state psychiatric hospital and, as a child, being surprised to see hordes of inmates pushing carts in the dry riverbed, forced by their guards to fill them with sand and roll them farther on, only to empty them into the water and begin again. This series of aberrant movements under a burning sun continued interminably, while, from time to time, one of the wretches threw himself screaming into the Loire...

In the same way, in the seventeenth century, for example, the La Charitè de Tours hospice must, like many others, partially renounce its silk industry before the threats of city manufacturers and limit its inmates to spooling and throwing silk threads.

At the same time, the chores imposed on the peasants are significantly broadened by the State, from carrying beggars to the hospice or the jail, to transporting men of war and criminals, whose fate is now similar. In the same way, this chore, which comes from the pact of feudal semi-colonization, was already a proletarianization, a mobilization of the peasant worker for the benefit of the logistical task—but again, in sub-working-class conditions.

Louis XIV one day declares to Colbert, "If you want to know what economy means, go to Flanders; you will see how little it costs to fortify conquered spaces." The King is alluding to the considerable earthworks and masonry undertaken by Louvois. Following the Roman example, he confided the execution of these works directly to the soldiers, all the while paying pitiful wages and maintaining military discipline.

Alongside the migrant's trajectory, there is the path of military proletarianization, the two having often been confused ever since Antiquity. Garlan evokes the roads and markets in which this specialized manpower gathered with its tribes and its races—in Cape Matapan south of the Peloponnesus, for example. Later, we will see the creation of an original logistical circuit necessitated by the increased recruitment of anational work forces by the committees or the *condottieri*—the famous Spanish road, compared by Parker to the Ho Chi Minh Trail. Along these trajectories they build temporary barracks. The beds are furnished by the villagers; they install health services similar to those of the hospice, required by the precarious living conditions of these wretches who escape jail or prison only to become soldiers again. Up until the nineteenth century, the barracks will be a kind of clinic in which venereal diseases and epidemics such as typhus will cause more deaths among the soldiers than battles and war wounds.

With conflicts of mass and of movement, death by exhaustion among the foot soldiers will take, says Chambray, frightening proportions. At the same time, they will notice a necessary evolution of the hospices that will recreate the unity of the mobile proletariat, as

Doctor Wasserthur notes in his report of June 10, 1884, on the condition of the Selestat hospital, in which diseased soldiers and war-wounded sleep alongside typhus cases, cancer patients and the destitute.

The social demands of the military proletariat will long remain the simple, vital requirements of subsistence: salaries, job security, on-the-job assistance to invalids and the wounded. Riots and mutinies take the form of frequent strikes, which are narrow in scope and generally concern delayed payment of wages—delays of up to ten years. The mutineers often form autonomous combat groups, electing a chief (Spanish *Electo*, German *ambosat*, etc.) who is assisted by a democratic council. And immediately these proletarian troops return to their initial demands. They try to take over and hold a fortification, to the point where their employers are finally obliged to concede, to pay what they owe so that the soldiers will get back on the highway. These limited revolts will nonetheless play an important role in the political evolution. For the satisfaction of the soldiers' demands helps, within the state apparatus, to hasten the development of the laboring and productive populations' material obligation toward those "luxury peoples" who supplant the old provincial masters. Tax, that economic vassalage, is sometimes levied directly by the soldiers, "an expedient means, disapproved of by Colbert who advises the collectors (as they then called those terrible animals) to use violence only as a last resort." Thus, the public treasury is able to maintain a standing army more decently, to counter frequent desertions by guaranteeing regular salaries. In this mitigated period, as Clausewitz shows, the military objective is accomplished with difficulty using money from the treasury. The vagabond troops are taken wherever they can be found, from one's own home or from the neighbor's, with no care for their past or their origins. Many able men at that time have no choice but to live as raiders, even as brigands, holding the countryside: "couriers riding onward, owing nothing while they are on the fields."

Since Babeuf and Engels, there has been much talk of the bodily mechanics of the proletarian soldier, of the obligation to serve the war machine, to carry out a repeated and invariable number of coordinated maneuvers (in the eighteenth century, for example, each shot fired from a cannon required about ten movements). Later they began wondering about the living conditions of the laboring proletariat—without, as did Engels, abandoning the disdain and repulsion that have surrounded the mobile mass of will-less bodies since time immemorial: the worker granted conditional freedom by the Chapelier Law during the French Revolution; the cloistered body of the woman, put in a harem or brothel ("*maison close*"), her sex sold or rented, even put under lock and key, as a source of profit for her temporary owner; bodies of the "forlorn hope"—the lost band—as the ideal object of training and discipline.

The "janissary" (the new soldier) is torn very young from the families of Christian slaves before undergoing military proletarianization. In the fifteenth century, the battles of Grandson and Morat show the importance the Swiss army attached to the presence of the forlorn hope, sent before the troops to fool the enemy; they are only hoodlums picked up in the city outskirts, miserable couriers doomed to certain death. Vauban, in the seventeenth century, states upon his return from an inspection tour that the Kingdom is put in danger "by those fortifications guarded by garrisons and squadrons of children, poor little wretches who are violently *abducted* from their homes or *stolen* in a thousand different ways." Abduction, kidnapping—the dromocrat's classic methods. It was therefore understandable that the military revolution of 1789 should legally put the proletariat of children to work.

In 1846 the *Revue des Deux Mondes* warns that in one year in France there were 32,000 cases of abandonment, or one child out of thirty deprived of his civil status, in other words of his *identity.* And Georges Sand, who is moved by this, describes in *The Country Waif* the procedure by which the child is confided to a traveler who takes him in a carriage and leaves him in the middle of a field. The loss of identity remains linked to exclusion from a geographic group, to setting a trajectory in motion, to putting on the road a child "who has not yet reached the age of reason."

There remains the difference between the "liberal" and the "mechanical," pure motivity, which comes from the machine and can thus be performed equally well by an ignoramus or an animal (Equicola 95): "manual labor being considered in the (anthropocentric) society of the Renaissance as ignoble as it had been in the Middle Ages," as Anthony Blunt notes in his *Artistic Theory in Italy, 1450–1600.* In fact, the worker's body cannot be compared to a human model, which is ideally composed. Vitruvian man is essentially reasonable and harmonious, since he is contained in the circles and grids of Euclidean geometry—a symbol of social superiority since it is the geometry of the invader's, the dominator's, trajectory.

It is curious to see current debates on the treatment, abandonment, slaughter and vivisection of animals, but also on the blockbuster movies in which a large number of them are sacrificed. In this context, let us quote the response of a stuntman, a "double," Mr. Dominique Zardi, who had been taken to task in a column entitled "The Martyrdom of the Animals," published in the newspaper *France Soir*: "Minor actors are in the same boat [as the animals]. They're also lesser members, shaken, bullied, cut off the screen...It's true I'm a tough little guy... But *no animal would have done what I've done, and I've never hurt one animal, woman or child,* since as everybody knows that's about the same thing."

The double's body, deprived of reason, is likened to that of other domestics, *in the same boat.* His work performances are here again absolutely compared to those of the animal by that dictator of movement, the film director. In ancient societies we know the bargains and ceremonies that surrounded the marriage of the "drudge-woman," consisting in exchanges of animals between the parties. In the armies and police forces the animal proletariat remains—the recent use of sea mammals being a modern example, a hold-over from the canine regiments trained for infantry combat. The vehicle-bodies of horses are likened in the Middle Ages to projectiles; the bodies of elephants to assault tanks, bulldozers, tractors; those of oxen, camels or mules are like jeeps. As for the pigeons, those predators, they are the media whose ownership is reserved for a social elite, itself predatory. The rapid information furnished by carrier pigeons allows Jacques Coeur to get richer on the stock markets, in particular the merchant marine. And it is striking to see the salt tax scale he kept in his Bourges hotel, a veritable trough designed to measure the tax on the cattle of "worker-producers" based on the quantity of salt they require as subsisting animal bodies—literally, the price of their sweat, since physical movement necessitates a salt consumption five times greater than that of the body in rest. Gandhi was to lead a far-reaching action in India against the English with respect to the salt tax, *as an economy of violence and slow death inflicted on the people colonized by the Western invader.* But still today, the most wide-spread conviction with respect to the bodies of those wanderers deprived of their identity, those living dead, is that they must be occupied, inhabited, possessed by wills other than their own, which is the very meaning of Frederick the Second's "Yours is not to reason why!" In the context of this disqualification of will in certain sexual, social or racial categories, it is significant to recall the conditions imposed on the descendants of the American black slaves, their battle for *civil rights*, particularly the right to vote which is but the "free man's" *right to want*, and which is not accorded to bodies without souls. In France the law of August 27, 1791 aggravates the tendency still further by requiring the elector to be a *landowner*: always the wandering body's inability to decide—inability of women, too, who will find it so hard to obtain the right to vote, to become part of this curious republican universalism!

We see here the social and political importance of "liberal reason" (of the open sea and open warfare) with respect not only to unreason but to the absence of reason pure and simple in the bodies of the ignorant, a relation faithfully reproduced as much in the Marxist organization chart as in the capitalist one, but at a lesser level…at least for the time being.

With the coming of democratic power, we see a perversion of primitive transmigration: the soul, by becoming individual, has become Reason, in other words the seat of a prescriptive rule of our actions, our movements, even the totality of our destinies. This reasoning nonetheless encounters resistance from the general confusion between common sense and the geometric hypothesis of *superior minds* (those of the military men Turenne and Vauban, or of bourgeois such as Colbert), as Moreau de Jonnes states in his *Social and Economic Status of France from 1589 to 1715.* Statistics care little about our long-term habits; and Vauban's derivation of 25,000 cases from one won't always be agreed with. But in the absence of cadastral investigation they still had to rely on inductive methods, arrived at by a rather crude approximation of notions of distribution. Later, Arthur Young, Chaptal and Lavoisier built their statistical tables on Vauban's inductive model, but with the difference that two out of three led to forecast errors. Further on, Moreau notes that Vauban's figures become easily understandable when *transformed into metric measurements...*

The soul neither preexists nor survives the disappearance of its body-vehicle or machine; but as potential Reason, and especially scientific Reason, it can act on foreign bodies which are distant in time and space. Animal, territorial, vegetable bodies, bodies without will, *bodies not yet born* become technical bodies or technological objects. Here is true social domination, the bestiary of engines. The purebred horse no longer acts, he is *acted on* by his rider thanks to the drive shaft of the bridle and the gas pedals of the spurs. Or else he takes the bit in his teeth, returns to his uncontrollable, wild state...he expresses himself!

Reason (as in the *Bible*) is, for the body, a form of death. Significantly, at the beginning of the Classical Age, the spectacle of the insane or possessed was fashionable, as is that of drug addicts today. We spy on the kinetic disorder of their inexplicable attitudes and their discourses. Even when he cries out, speaks or complains, the possessed one, like the animal, is supposed not to suffer, and thus cannot be an object of pity. Whence the judicial, then "medical," arsenal of treatments inflicted daily on these soulless bodies by their owners, executioners, judges or doctors: burns, injections, ripping out of fingernails and hair, and finally electro-shock. The body is an empty house through which pass disquieting tenants, if one is not careful—a house best made as uncomfortable as possible. Still today, psychoanalysis practically realizes these beliefs by claiming to bring *the unconscious* back to *the expression of a reasonable consciousness*. But more than houses, these bodies are *metabolic vehicles*.

And the pseudo-demons that we try to extract from them are primarily intelligences—themselves in transit—that abusively occupy the "driver's seat," like a horseman (again) who, controlling the back of his horse, claims to have its "motor at his disposal."

Foreign "intelligences" breathe into the vacant body an inhabitual dynamism, commanding it to perform corresponding gestures. Ancient metempsychosis imagined a plethora of intelligences in search of undifferentiated matter. The movement of transmigration supposedly takes place naturally, notably at birth and death, into any body at all, thus creating a kind of physical equality that surpasses social organizations. Another remark: when the landworker is transformed into a conqueror, the population's poetic potential disappears in favor of a military potential, the poetic transmigration of souls disappears in favor of conquest, in other words of the voyage of bodies, and thus of their deterritorialization, of their inequality. With reasonable possession, the *boarding* of the metabolic vehicle is literally an act of piracy. Doctor Claude Olivenstein speaks of psychoanalysis as "psychism's strongest and most important *lever of penetration*": always the unconscious reference to violence and to the right of the "power to invade, to its mechanical techniques. After all is said and done, the Russian psychiatrists, accused of violence by their colleagues during a 1977 colloquium, might well be the most faithful to the ethics of their arts. Otherwise we get repression and discipline *à la* Skinner, or Sakol's cures for drug addiction. As Olivenstein notes, "They no longer take drugs, but they *wander like shadows*"—living dead ever ready to welcome unusual transients.

The social staging of human love was perhaps one of the last poetic manifestations of the fluidiform soul, occasionally incarnated. The brutal unveiling of the sexual act—sex education or pornography

—as technical revelation is another way of boarding "ignorant" bodies, the logical next step from the gymnasium: the famous physical culture, "Swedish style," is succeeded by the modern mixture of highway and sex, bodies thrown together by chance meetings; sexual collisions soon forgotten; autos, motorcycles stolen, raped and abandoned.[2]

"Good conduct" is no longer *morals* taught in public school, but driver's education, which is becoming an obligatory part of the curriculum.[3] But isn't this already the adventure of military monasticism, transforming the mystical body of Christ into an armed body, into marching orders?

Long before pirates, assault troops or hoodlums, the military monk finds gratification in the arsenal of death and terror. In fact, if the militarization of societies henceforth makes every citizen *a war machine*, the soldier-monk is, in this domain, a model and a precursor. The reform of the great orders, aimed at suppressing the military Gyrovagues, is a considerable revolution, since the monk's "solitude" is now spread to large, anational armed groups. The institution of monastic autism in the very nature, time, space, and social and human organizations that he relinquishes, his renunciation of personal tastes and identity, prefigure the nihilism of the technological revolution spoken of by Heidegger. The monk, voluntarily absent from himself, sworn to silence, chastity and especially obedience, becomes the vehicle of his "director" of conscience (the drive shaft that powers "order," a superior and universal "Reason").

We know that monasticism is more a military invention than a religious one; we find it in every part of the world. Since antiquity, whenever the notion of State has developed, military sects have multiplied at the same time. It is no surprise that Hegel's concept of the modern State was born in Prussia, former home of the

Teutonic Order, which was secularized in 1525. It was the *carbonari*, with their "cellular" organization, who became a model for other revolutionary groups, the clandestine movements that in Russia were the axes of a systematized terrorist war, of a permanent nihilism comparable both to the permanent war led by the great orders—first against the Muslims, then, in America, against the Asians—and then the guerrilla war led against Napoleon in Spain... Dugesclin, the secret master of the military Temple, had excelled there just as well.[4] In the same way, puritanism and industrialization progress together in Anglo-Saxon countries. With industrial internment, it is redemptive to put the soulless bodies of children and women to work because these bodies are guided by reasonable souls, the souls of engineers assigned to define their attitudes and gestures. *Arbeit macht frei*: Nazi and Chinese re-education camps claim this old kinetic belief for themselves.

In these different examples, the conqueror, the warrior claims a function that seems to be a perversion of the priest's. For the Judeo-Christians, everything is said from the very first pages of the *Bible: the warrior is a perverted priest.* In fact, the first murder revolves around the means of occupying and exploiting productive soil, and especially around the rent received by God in exchange. God willingly accepts the sacrifice paid by the shepherd Abel but refuses that of the farmer Cain. The image of the first killer of men bears a direct relation to *the rent paid on the earth*, and here again everything is said in several lines: the *suffering* of the soil "opening its mouth" and crying out as it drinks human blood for the first time—the blood of the territorial body as it slips away. (It shall no longer yield to you its fruit, says God...you will be a *wanderer* crossing over and invading the earth.) Deterritorialized farmer, the first killer of men is immediately designated a *builder of cities* (a commoner).

The importance of the priest (the magician), of the patriarch, comes from his ability to establish and maintain this commerce of exchange with the gods/nature, to temper their whims, their violence. He is the one who, thanks to his scientific empiricism, can make them accept his sacrifice, the rent on the earth (he collects, sets and levies the tax, tithe or—in its current manifestation—church-offering). When, with the advent of the "foreigner," a commerce of transferable goods is instituted on the banks of the Mediterranean, it is curious to see the exchange take place in a similar way (as still happens today with certain nomads): without any physical or even visual contact between the two parties. The merchandise is deposited on the shore or the side of the road, where the stranger will pick it up, put in its place the appointed value, and then leave. He thus passes like a shadow over the other's territory, scarcely setting foot on it, like those souls, those wills that occupy the invisible or uninhabitable parts of the universe. The colonial godowns and free ports still reproduce, in their way, this process of exchange existing outside of military conventions. The warrior, dromocratic killer and organizer of crossroad-cities, has from the dawn of history concentrated all his effort and science on exacting rent for the earth. Armed force is always one of military occupation, and it is at this level that the warrior appears as a perverted priest. Curiously, total war and the nuclear stand-off tend to bring him back to his original role. In fact, the principle of deterrence is not only a strategic formula, but is also the earth's inhabitants finally paying their rent, literally reaching the *term* (limit and end).

The expatriate warrior, building the world-wide nuclear enclosure, is in a position to demand an exorbitant rent from populations that have become entirely native, given the current proportions of "the meter covered, protected." The function of the hero—military protector and tax collector—can thus in no way be limited to or even identified with "human commerce," as Clausewitz understands it, for instance. The warrior's or soldier-monk's abuse of the earth's (divine) hospitality is not only the acquisition or accumulation of soil and riches in the name of a State of which he is but the instrument (the lever, as Saint-Just says!), but is all of that as the indefinite expansion of the abuse itself. Moreover, we find this clearly mimed by the *great* conquerors: Alexander is content to move forward, worried only about *reaching a limit* and thus an end to his power of penetration. If Frederick the Second declares that "to win is to advance," Napoleon states that he wants *to found and not to possess.* Conquest is reduced to quest; gesture is movement. Napoleon will die poor, like a soldier monk, in the little grey outfit that, on the battlefield, set him apart from his officers and gaudy, mercenary generals, designating the "detached" character he intended for his military art. Perverted priests—Muslim, Christian or otherwise—developing the arsenal of war alongside the inferno, mixing poverty with the "hatred of the world."

Financial politics are exercised around the abduction of persons, ransom systems; social protection leads to the perversion of charity into bodily assistance, of poverty into the power of money—to such an extent that when these great mechanisms stop functioning profitably, the Roman papacy of monks collapses. Its system of military security goes along with its system of social security, the Inquisition with its temporal power. It is the same for the *great* conquerors: they are all lost as soon as they must renounce the raping of nations. All greatness lies in Assault, in the dimension borrowed from distance. War is assault, because war is the permanent abuse of the earth's hospitality, its penetration. Here, once again, we must look at the speedometer of the racing engine, the combat racecar: an existential measure of the warrior's being, the dizzying flow of time, a rapidity-tax on the covered meter that ruins the earthly inhabitant, but simultaneously destroys the substance of its conqueror and measures the survivor's remaining hours.[5] In short, as in the turnaround of the topological ring, the survivor's disappearance depends on the answer he can give in space and time to Alexander the Great's question, to the problem of his limits.[6]

The invader's performance resembles that of his athletic counterpart, of those olympic champions whose records first progressed by hours, then by minutes, then by seconds, then by fractions of seconds. The better they performed (the more rapid they became), the more pitiful were the advances they obtained, until they could only be noticed electronically. One day the champion will disappear in the limits of his own record, as is already suggested by the biological manipulation of which he is the object, and which resembles the methods of artificial medical survival granted the terminally ill. For the dromomaniac the engine is also a prosthesis of survival. It is remarkable that the first automobiles, Joseph Cugnot's military trolley of 1771, for example, were steam-powered, already situating themselves at the limit of the animal body's metempsychosis, relay of historical evolution: the limit of the passage from the metabolic vehicle to the technological vehicle, spilling its smoke like a last breath, a final symbolic manifestation of the motor-power of living bodies.

3

The End of the Proletariat

> *You can have a proletarian insurrection on the condition that the others hold their fire. If they dump two tank battalions on you, the proletarian revolution is as good as nothing.*
>
> — Andre Malraux, *Interviews*

EVIDENTLY, DROMOLOGICAL progress and what we conventionally call human and social progress coincided but did not converge. The development can be summarized as follows:

1. A society without technological vehicles, in which the woman plays the role of the logistical spouse, mother of war and of the truck.

2. The indiscriminate boarding of soulless bodies as metabolic vehicles.

3. The empire of speed and technological vehicles.

4. The metabolic vehicle competing with, then defeated by, the earthly technological vehicle.

We could logically conclude with a last paragraph:

5. The end of the dictatorship of the proletariat and of History in the war of Time.

If we come back to Goebbels' definition, or Engels', the invention of the militant—revolutionary worker or otherwise—already makes for no more than a "poor man's" version of the proletarian soldier. The proletarianization of the working classes is only one form of militarization—a temporary form.

From 1914 onward, the proletariat's motor—and thus political—power was no match for the European battlefields. This power, however, was still indispensable to the worksites of continental warfare. The military class, making sure to keep the proletariat under control, will thus allow it the illusion of being able to dominate, to submerge the bourgeois fortress. The latter is already ruined, pierced at all points by the expressway media (radio, telephone, television), condemned by its former defenders to instant destruction through the anti-city strategy of total war. Nonetheless, we will soon become familiar with the limits of this *military leave*, in Prague, Warsaw, Beirut...and in Paris, too, in May '68, when, after the taking of the Odeon theatre, the government predicts at any moment the intervention of armored cars against the popular uprising. It is understandable that in the 1920s, while the "Bolshevik threat" spread from Munich to the gates of India, the French government unleashed a new politics of social aid. All this was made necessary by the logistical redeployment of military-industrial nations in Europe and in the world. And yet everyone is surprised to discover that in Part XIII of the Preamble to the Treaty of Versailles it says that "the living conditions of the working classes"—of "the balance of military forces in the world" would be more appropriate!—"are incompatible with world peace."

This is the new mix that Junger partially reveals a little later, in 1932, in his essay *Der Arbeiter* (the figure of the worker encompasses the soldier and the industrialist), a work that was to win a large audience and rapidly become for the Germans a veritable political platform...

In the same way, the French Union of the Left is a trap insofar as it has insisted, in General Cluseret's words, on having "the army constitute an unknown quantity in the social equation." In short, its only strength has been its silence on the military question. It is inevitable that its undoing will be the problem of national Defense, and that the Communists, who have always accepted the Marxist model of military proletarianization, will find themselves confronting radicals and socialists who, since May 1968, have invested in a socialism "with a human face," liable to assemble a new, somewhat depoliticized electorate. It was under the auspices of the Portugese generals of the Armed Forces Movement that "the end of the dictatorship of the proletariat" was decreed in Southern Europe. We should not see in this, as Georges Marchais will later claim, a cause for rejoicing, a softening of ideological will, "the word 'dictatorship' having an unpleasant sound since the fascist experience." Indeed, we cannot accuse the Portugese military leaders—returning to their country after a long and bloody campaign of colonial repression—of excessive humanism. In fact, with the Marxist generals courted by Cunhal, the dictatorship of the proletariat regains its original military significance; and as good technicians of war, they acknowledge that the time when the proletariat's kinetic energy dominated political life, after having dominated the battlefield, is reaching an end—the time when, as Lenin says, the working class suddenly found itself courted and solicited even by the capitalists.

From now on, the animal body of the worker is devalued as the bodies of other domestic species were before him. The end of the dictatorship of the proletariat is only the Communist version of facts already noted—by the French army, for example, when they did away with the review board (law of July 9, 1970), or in 1975, on the liberal side, by the "Trilateral Commission" on the crisis of democracy: "We have come to recognize that if there are potentially desirable limits to economic growth, there are also potentially desirable limits to the infinite expansion of democracy." The crisis of these liberal democracies is the end of a form of mobilization of the citizenry. The central historical pseudo-figure of the dominating producer is simultaneously removed by the two great ideological blocs, the proletarian worker declared unusable along with the consumer-producer of the capitalist world. The revolutionary experiment of the Armed Forces Movement was in this context exemplary because it claimed to raise the Portugese leftist forces to another level, that of an "army civilization." Thus in 1975, ship's captain Correia Jesuino, who had become "Minister of Social Communication" (we are reminded here of the naval proletarianization under Louis XIV by M. de Valbelle, the former captain of the galleys), depicts the "left wing" officers as "ethnologists studying a primitive people." For, in his view, the Portugese people is underdeveloped. Jean Francois Revel, reporting these statements in *L'Express* (April 14, 1975), indicated that the average salary of a Portuguese was comparable to that of a Breton or a Welshman, and didn't quite see where the "underdevelopment" was.

All of this, indeed, is inexplicable in economic terms; instead we must emphasize a dromological military philosophy that challenges everyone's participation in a state totality, making this participation problematic. In the same way, if the nuclear problem in 1977 caused the French Union of the Left to break apart, it was less a matter of megatons than of *the political vectors of the new nuclear power*. Without our realizing it, *the nuclear weapon logically modified the political constitution of the States in the world.* As one lawyer put it, "We must recognize that the nuclear weapon has shown itself to be a source of constitutional right by modifying our actual constitution."

Here again, it is not so much the final explosion that counts in deterrence; rather more it is questions such as those posed by Articles 5 and 15 of the French Constitution of 1958 to the solitary decision maker that the Head of State and Supreme Commander of the Armies, the President of the Republic, guarantor of the national territory's integrity, has become. The speed of the political decision depends on the sophistication of the vectors: how to transport the bomb? how fast? The bomb is political, we like to repeat—political not because of an explosion that should never happen, but because it is the ultimate form of military surveillance.

The political bourgeoisie, like the "revolutionary" parties, anesthetized by a long period of coexistence and full employment, by the euphoria of continued growth, are proving in Europe that "one can do anything with a bayonet except sit on it." The proletarian revolution now *necessarily* goes through the revolutions of the military institutions in the heart of the State's constitutional apparatus and, in fact, the principal actors who have taken the initiative these last years are no longer the great political parties, but the army, the unions, and even the unions in the army.

It is useful to notice here the anational nature of these events. For if one of the French national labor unions (the C.F.D.T.) wholeheartedly supports military unionism, requesting a "body politic of the soldier," at the same time the famous A.F.L.-C.I.O. has declared itself ready to take the American soldiers' unions under *its* wing. Here something fundamental is happening, which no one has clearly pointed out: a non-partisan dialogue is being created between the world's labor forces and the military class and, in the short term, a "latinization" of Europe comparable to that of the South American continent. If General Vargas Prieto, "considered one of the most capable and progressive leaders in the Peruvian army" (*Le Monde*, November 4, 1975), declares in an interview that "the true forerunners of the Peruvian revolution are its armed forces, the root and *institutional essence of the people because they are born from them,*" we must understand that this really means a return to a situation that long precedes political Marxism, to a negation of the State-polis by the proletarian revolutionary forces.

Le Monde reported in August 1977 that General Pinochet had done away with the DINA, his political police, in favor of a military police force. Things are getting simpler... This is truly the end of the reasonable democratic State that engages in a non-partisan process in which the unions and the most disparate, the least "socialized" groups, are called to play the primary role. We are heading toward an explosion of national production systems, toward union individuation as it exists in the United States, for example—human labor depending less on productivity than on the game of interests in the manpower market. This, along with the breakdown of the unity of political action, allows for every imaginable maneuver, even the wildest and most fragmented, on the level of the very survival of the old political States. The end of democracy in Chile was thus foreseen and orchestrated by the CIA, and pressure was exerted on the highway systems by the truckers' unions, telecommunications, etc.

But what should we think of the crisis situation in the old urban fortresses, in New York or Montreal? The union functions, relayed by mob associations, are entirely supplanting the administration and services of the old bourgeois employer. Order reigns in the Bronx thanks to the Mafia, which is itself becoming international, aiming now at a direct collaboration with the military class, as was revealed by a recent scandal that called into question the relations between the Israeli generals and members of international crime. Far from being a military political function that is becoming deterritorialized, losing interest in any form of sedentary fixation, whether national or otherwise, both the petty criminals and the large gangs are seeing their local cottage industry undergo serious revaluation.

The military class, increasingly distanced from its bourgeois partner, abandons the street, the highway, those outmoded vectors, to the small and middle-sized business of the protection rackets. The city unions in New York are starting to replace their members' productive activity with simple crisis management, by becoming administrators and bankers.

In Italy, assassinations, abductions, crimes and incidents are on the rise. Financial interests are becoming inseparable from those of a multitude of little, so-called "revolutionary," groups. Justice is in a quandary. They talk about "liberating the people" and extort millions from them. Public opinion is in an uproar about the mix, but this criminal power rising from the masses is really only *a political demand* returning to an uncontrolled condition because the old national ethology—social ideals—has become secondary and no longer mobilizes.

We can thus interpret the unexpected visits of political leaders such as Messrs. Marchais and Chevenement to the workers in their offices and factories not as a challenge to the bosses or the government, but as unavowed attempts by the representatives of the devalued revolutionary ideologies to take the grass roots back in hand. While the Communist Party in Portugal completely failed in its opportunistic attempts with the military masters, the French Communist Party, once hesitant, seemed to approach the courageous

Italian solution of Mr. Berlinguer, whose famous "historical compromise" really only means a final, desperate union of the traditional parties before the threat of pure and simple disappearance that weighs on them from both within and without.

While in France they try to keep the masses tied to outmoded strategic and social convictions, the army is already deploying its personnel in key points of civilian activity and shadows the police in its surveillance tasks. The military proletariat's job is henceforth to police highways and airports, to collect garbage on public roads (where men like Democrat Abraham Beame, New York's "little mayor," was ridiculed), as well as to provide telecommunications and assistance; to effect certain prestige operations such as the battle against pollution, campaigns for the defense of archeological sites or cancer research, the organization of numerous athletic and cultural displays (Celebration in the Tuileries, the army at the Children's Fair); and to accomplish important international enterprises, such as saving children in Biafra, setting up surgical units in areas devastated by natural cataclysms… even "rescuing" a group of hostages in Entebbe. In a threatening social universe, in which human societies are shown to be rife with criminal elements, the army seems to be a protective force, a refuge from the parade of subversive enterprises. The army continues to be greatly amused by the "anti-militarists'" lack of information about, and static analysis of, its dynamic power.

The army's answer to the ecological celebration in Larzac, the Melville tragedy, was *Operation Demeter*, "named for the Greek goddess who personified the Earth." Why did they have to call it "Demeter?" why did they present themselves as occupiers and dominators of the planet Earth? why did they violate and damage the fields?—unless the Larzac celebration had claimed, albeit inadvertently, to frustrate them in their primary function, the power to invade? Why was it that at that very moment the "friends of the earth" lost contact with their planet, and haven't even demonstrated any resistance? In any case, the terminology used by Jacques Isnard in the September 9, 1977 issue of *Le Monde* gives us pause: "Between the end of the harvest and the opening of the hunting season, the *land* army organized, in the Beauce and Perche regions, its first true maneuver in *open ground*, in other words, *away from the highways and roads*, in a region of 2,000 square kilometers of farm land and prairies." They put on a "show maneuver" in order to maintain *neighborly relations between the army and the civilian populations*. The farmers, who remembered the army's help during the previous year's drought, accepted the Demeter exercise without, it seems, too much grumbling… "Goddess Demeter is with us," recognizes Colonel de Rochegonde, who commands the 2nd Motor Brigade. While another colonel states, "We are but the *managers* of national Security and, as such, we too are held accountable." "The army takes advantage of these maneuvers in open ground to lead, for example, offensive reconnaissance missions fifty kilometers from its base, along with *public relations* operations in the Eureet-Loire department." You do not enclose dromocrats in gulags or camps, not even in Larzac.

The Institute of Advanced Studies in National Defense spent six months in collaboration with advertising experts setting up a three-year campaign (at a cost of sixty million francs) aimed at sensitizing the public to the notion of defense and protection, using every means of information at their disposal to change the army's image (*Le Monde,* May 9, 1975).

Joel le Theule, Gaullist deputy and chairman of the Finance Committee, thus has reason to worry, in his notes on "the military budget for 1977-1982," about "the absence of numerical information on the use of funds"; for this *fuzziness* allows no appreciation of the shifts in our defense policies. The army insists on regaining its autonomy of action, on redefining itself as *a public service able to assume in a safe and orderly fashion* the greatest number—even the totality—of civil and military defense tasks, again increasing the communal and industrial undertakings of its parallel initiatives. We can thus see just how far military unionism, advocated by the Communist League, the Unified Socialist Party or the C.F.D.T. in the name of petty demands, finally enters into the army's social scheme. It is, moreover, revealing to see the creation of the first union branch in the 19th Army Engineering Corps, thus demonstrating that this body still remains at the forefront of military revolutionary thought!

Balzac, visiting the Wagram battlefield after 1830 in hopes of *expanding his social analysis*, already asked himself the *question of the veritable territory of historiality*, the strategic theatre that, thanks to the advance of the media (the use of the telegraph, for example), had suddenly become global—external and internal events henceforth able to interact almost immediately. This temporal limitation come from the battlefield had been answered by the new "secret police," which Balzac considers the most important social revolution of his time—the moment when, after the long period of ostensible and bloody repression exerted against the civilian populations by the Revolution's "army of the interior," military violence stops being necessarily visible only from afar, by the soldier's uniform, and comes to rest on refined systems of surveillance and denunciation.

These first attempts at penetration, clandestine "invasion" of the social corpus, had, as we saw, a specific aim: exploitation by the armed forces of the nation's raw potential (its industrial, economic, demographic, cultural, scientific, political and moral capabilities). Since then, social penetration has been linked to the dizzying evolution of military penetration techniques; each vehicular advance erases a distinction between the army and civilization.

Fascism, defining itself in Germany as *Ostkolonisation*, in other words the institution of a colonial situation on the European continent that claims to subvert existing socio-political groups, in fact reveals to us the great two-way movement of dromocratic totalitarianism between metropoles and colonies. Mapped out during the unprecedented logistical effort of the First World War, this movement will bring about the singular unity of Western civilization in the 1920s, "the incorporation of colonial action in national life as a solution to the serious problems that human evolution will later impose on the world," as Albert Sarraut, French colonial minister, declared in 1921.

To understand dromocratic society and its establishment, it is no doubt more useful to read *The Black Code* of the Colonial Pact than any other so-called sociological work. "We must not," wrote Colbert, "constitute in the colonies a *constant* civilization." The ancient legislation that will subsist in our colonies until 1848 considers the negro to be *furniture*;[1] the black slave is first of all a *movable commodity*. His legal existence is solely a function of his movable/furniture quality, of the transportation he is subjected to. The vogue of Black American jazz after 1914, the frenzied gesticulation revealed by the first American sound film that colored the face of a white actor and bent him to the rhythm of the movable slave, reminds us of that country's dominant culture today, and of James Baldwin's profound reflection: "Tomorrow you will all be negroes!"

In fact, from the beginning, the American system has not had a measure of comparison between the value of the messages delivered and the effort necessary for their transmission. More so than with the content of the message, the means of its mediatization appear as instruments of primary necessity in the United States, first of all in their naval relation to metropolitain Europe, to the Africa that supplies its manpower, then for the constitution of a certain State centralism over a vast territory in which, in order to govern, one must first penetrate and then communicate.

The media are the privileged instruments of the Union. They alone are able to control the social chaos of American pan-humanity; they are the guarantors of a certain civic cohesion, and thus of civil security itself. Inversely, as in the ancient colonial model, American democracy will make no real efforts to integrate its ethnic minorities, its factions, into a constant civilization, into a truly community-oriented way of life. For segregation is what sanctions the system's hegemony of the media, on which rests the nature of the American State's authority.

This is one reason for the survival of old racism among the *good citizens* of the "land of the free;" and we will note as well that the great internal and external upheavals in the United States will be linked directly to dromological events, to the very techniques of penetration and transmission—from the delayed radio message of Pearl Harbor to the affair of the Watergate microphones or the Kennedy assassination: we could draw up a list. *Citizen Kane*, the most accomplished product of American civic culture (later baptized "pop-culture!"), is less William Randolph Hearst, the newspaper magnate who served as Orson Welles' model, than Howard Hughes, the invisible citizen. Hearst still delivered information; Hughes was content to speculate indifferently on whatever delivered it. He singlehandedly constituted the most radical critique of Fuller's and MacLuhan's global theories. This completely desocialized man, who vanished from the earth, who avoided human contact for fear of germs, who was terrified by the very breath of his rare visitors, nonetheless thought only of the media, from the aerospace industry to the cinema, from gasoline to airfields, from casinos to the star system, from the design of Jane Russell's bra to that of a bomber. His existence could be considered exemplary. Hughes cared only about that which passes in transit. His life rebounded from one vector to another, as has, for two hundred years, the power of the American nation he adored. Nothing else interested him. He died in the open sky, in an airplane.

In the same way, American commercial methods triumphed in Europe in 1914 thanks to the unforeseen logistical dimensions taken by the conflict. The United States was to win on the continent one of the first gasoline wars, putting the French market in the hands of Standard Oil, driving back our army which had gone to the front with 400 tanker trucks while the Americans owned more than 20,000. Once more, the market was created not by the object of consumption but by its vector of delivery!

Once peace was restored, it is interesting to see America retreat from the European market, notably from France, where the company representatives were unable to effectively implant their products, "having committed gross psychological errors in their advertising campaigns." To speak plainly, European culture still victoriously resists American cultural overthrow. We will see totalitarian governments try to install comparable vectors. But, being-all-too often tangled up in elitist culture and used to giving more importance to the message than to the vehicle, they will have difficulty, using ideological propaganda, in attaining the perfect logistical efficiency of the American patriotic "short-cut."

Later, after total war—in other words after the extensive destruction of the European nations' identity (total war, like colonial war, aiming at the annihilation of constant civilizations)—we see the evacuation of American stocks toward Europe. But here again, we haven't sufficiently analyzed this flow of instruments and objects brought over by the *liberty ships.* We must still apply aesthetic, functional and other meanings to this world of giant cars; to the plethora of household objects in gleaming kitchens in which, significantly, nothing is cooked but sandwiches and canned foods; to the whole spectacle of a "thoughtless objectivity that makes the very concept of consciousness meaningless;" to the clandestine interference in the ordinary vectors of exchange and communication by the technological codes that result from production systems.

Technologies of body and soul are thus strangely complexified in American pop-culture. The body without soul is, as we saw, a body assisted by technical prostheses. And since we're talking about America, we would do well to remember that the word "comfort" comes from the old French *assistance*: a reference to the old social bestiary of bodies seized in motion, left along the road. Unleashed in the 1920s, the de-neutralization of the media paves the way for what has been called "the war of the domestic market," a massive ideological campaign addressed directly to the family puzzle that it claims to put together, even to reinvent, as an "infinite receptacle for consumer goods."[2] This campaign will very quickly become a veritable animal domestication of the American citizen.

Significantly, the American government will not deem it necessary to establish a veritable welfare system on its own territory. It is convinced at the time that the promotion of a paternalistic and humanitarian *comfort* civilization will perfectly replace social aid through the *technical assistance of bodies*, from the household robot to the company psychiatrist or the latest model of car. Not unlike the way this country today nurtures a romantic taste for the revived bionic bodies of fascistic futurism, human bodies in which certain organs have been replaced by technological grafts, enabling these new heroes of surgical science to accomplish superhuman physical exploits.

But the politics of comfort was superseded by that of *social standing.* Everyone suddenly found himself exposed to the scrutiny of his neighbors, compared with the Identikit portrait of the ideal American consumer: a model of civic-mindedness whose gestures, quirks and attitudes toward life were henceforth broadcast without reprieve by the radio, the press, television and the cinema, and buried under commercial messages. Its political counterpart is the McCarthy period, a time of blacklisting, of anti-American witch hunts, of artists and intellectuals on trial—the same artists and intellectuals who were again designated in 1975 by the Trilateral Commission as a threat to democracy by their ability to constitute demobilized and irredeemable margins.

In fact, American-style (social) security implies the population's cultural underdevelopment. It is remarkable to see modern democratic States bragging about their *silent majorities.* In its way, the silence of the American people has become just as oppressive as that of the Russian people; social standing has become a step toward the invention of the proletarian policeman.

The hierarchy of high speeds of penetration and assault made and unmade the specter of the proletarian as if in a lap-dissolve—that mutation that begins with the all-too clear social distribution commanded by the Convention, then continues with the cloudier look of Marx and Engels, who are unable to see the mythic figure of the Worker, even in the rich deposit of industrial proletarianization that is England in the nineteenth century. Engels cannot find his *specimen*, his neanderthal of historical evolution...[3] Only in June 1848 will the image finally take shape, in the streets of Paris, on a theatre of civil war "as populated as that of the Battle of Leipzig," where thirty to forty thousand men are thrown into combat.

Just as the revolutionary process of the proletarianization of labor comes from the war of mass and movement, the myth of "the worker of metaphysics" (Biblical image of man's first pain: cursed by God and cursing and killing in turn to replace Him in His creative works) also *takes shape* on the great battlefields of industrial war. Teilhard de Chardin, for example, believes along with most of his contemporaries that war is one of the principle ferments of technological progress; but the idea of "unfinished man" suddenly strikes him during his "unforgettable experience at the front," as he writes in 1917. In 1945, at the end of the total war, he notes, "War is an *organic phenomenon of anthropogenesis* that Christianity cannot suppress any more than it can do away with death." He adopts the voice of Tacitus to deplore the international Peace that will cover the world with "the crust of banality, the veil of monotony" (*La nostalgie du front*, 1917). "Something like a light will go out over the earth." *Demobilization* will be, for the member of the "Yellow Crusade" (that epic of automotive assault), *immobilization* in anti-revolution-evolution.

While preparation for war requires months, even years, the decisive assault lasts only an hour, perhaps only a few minutes. Something of the evolutionary-revolutionary gaze on bodies engaged in historical kineticism is held over from the fatal homosexuality of ancient generals, enlightened despots and sultans, who would force the "militias that are very pleasant to watch, if you are not the one to receive the blows" to repeat their maneuvers endlessly.[4] Each is seized by an immoderate desire for the subjected flesh of the proletarian soldier, the powerful mass of "mobile machines...blindly obeying the impulses of their drivers" (Babeuf). The military work-forces are obliged not so much to sell themselves as to *give* themselves to the war entrepreneur. For him they are what the woman, then the mount, was for the knight in battle: they help him move forward, die under him or cause his death. Alexander is nothing without the humors of Bucephalus; Richard the Third at Bosworth loses his life—and his kingdom—along with his horse. The military, then laboring, proletarian kinetic, infinite, prolifically self-regenerating—carries into time and space the historical guide who straddles him, directs and inspires his movements, and who is also a chief of war: Lenin, Trotsky, Stalin, Mao.

In short, the revolutionary figure of the worker, sketched less by the industrial system than by the military one, fills the kinetic disparity between slow war and rapid war. The "full steam ahead through the mud" of the nihilist Nechaiev, apostle of systematized terrorist warfare, is not a rhetorical figure but a serious technological proposition: compensate for the distortion born of the destructive assault's necessary brevity by accelerating the rhythm of attacks. Historical evolution is then kept moving literally *by a combustion engine!*

German fascism will have the same concerns. With Heidegger it becomes "*die Totale Mobil-Machung*," "the final stage of the will to power and the realization of the essence of technology: nihilism." The proletarian soldier can in non-war pursue his revolutionary task, assault, which has become an aggression against nature. This is the pan-destruction of the world (Bakunin), the great geo-political sites that devote the earth to war, keeping its *visible surface* for the "worker of metaphysics," or giving it to him by educating him. In practice, this begins as a kind of humanitarian aid to the German unemployed, then as a voluntary service to which Heidegger calls the intellectuals, "a service of work, knowledge and arms." This will become the exemplary development of the history of the camps that, in 1926, receive their first volunteers, mixing, in the most moving manner possible, workers, peasants and students.

The whole thing could have seemed extremely liberal at a time when, everywhere in the Western world, a crushing need for manpower was being felt. The insatiable requirements of industrial warfare, already forgotten after so few years, simultaneously put the populations to work and domesticated them with para-military State bureaucracies in Europe, across the Atlantic and overseas (between the two wars, moreover, the International Labor Office in Geneva handled all of the world's manpower problems).

In the colonies, American "forcing" is answered by the *smotig*, the organization of penal labor; while in Bulgaria, for example, civilian labor is made obligatory from 1920 onward, for both sexes, under a general office attached to the Ministry of Public Works. But the beneficiaries usually work on construction projects headed by the Ministry of War: strategic roads, railways, airports, factories.

The fascist project as well, in the final account, is no more than a compromise in the conflict that has long opposed, in the heart of the State, the aristocracy, the military class and the bourgeoisie, each one fighting over its proletariat. In Germany, labor service will be made mandatory in 1928; those who try to avoid it become objects of scorn, social exclusion or denunciation, as the deserter or shirker was in time of war. In 1934, the completely standardized work camps become detention camps; and they will be transformed into concentration camps, into death camps, in the face of public apathy, without anyone even bothering to remove their original motto: "Arbeit macht frei."

The slip from one to the other is in fact quite natural; the proletarian worker's flesh is no different from that of the proletarian soldier. As Clausewitz writes: "Tools (soldiers) are there to be used, and use will naturally wear them out..."

For their part, the Communist countries ostensibly fulfilled Teilhard de Chardin's wish at the very moment he formulated it: *die Totale Mobil-Machung*. More than the suppression of the bourgeois class, this is the disappearance of its productive proletariat. In China, from 1964 onward, the revolutionary slogan was "Take the army as your model"; and the entire population was forced to wear a similar uniform, a kind of ambiguous, asexual outfit. In France, on the other hand, the soldier was called upon more and more frequently to wear the combat uniform, the outfit of the laborer, even during official parades.

All greatness is in assault!—an inaccurate translation of Plato or a paraphrasing of American forcing?[5] Fascism was totalitarian only insofar as it intended to be totally dromocratic. The "vital space" is only the disappearance of European geography, become an area, a desert without qualities, expanded by a "social" organization made entirely functional by the hierarchy of speed—the same hierarchy that had produced National Socialism on the streets of Berlin, before returning with total war to its elitist cultural origins. From the beginning, the superb body of the Man of Assault, of the blond and naturalistic Aryan, is willingly exhibited by Nazi propaganda. What the Berlin stadium's celebration of the olympic liturgy shows is a hierarchy of bodies according to speeds of penetration. The athletic body is prytanic—projectile or projector. The excitement of the speed or distance record is that of assault. This *countdown in time and space*, the very principle of athletic performance, is but the theatricalization of the race toward its "absolute greatness," of that military charge that begins as a slow and geometric march, and continues as an increasingly powerful acceleration of the body meant to give the final surge.

With total war, the "*Totale Mobil-Machung*" takes on its full meaning. There is no longer any social comparison between the triumphant body of the proletarian soldier—the superior being who, according to the old expression, possesses the "magnificence of displacement;" the German soldier who rushes headlong into the limitless expanse of the steppe or the desert—and the body of the proletarian worker who is there only to support the logistical effort. A mass of the physically unfit, of forced residents, of prisoners interned in camps, unable bodies, petty criminals…

For the Italian fascist passing directly from the athletic record to absolute war, the intoxication of the speed-body is total; it's Mussolini's "Poetry of the bomber." For Marinetti, after d'Annunzio, the "warrior-dandy" is the "only able subject, *surviving* and savoring in battle the power of the human body's metallic dream"; coupling with technological equipment scarcely more cumbersome than a horse, the old metabolic vehicle of the warring elites: rapid launches or "torpedos" straddled under the sea by aristocratic frogmen in search of the British fleet. The Japanese kamikaze will realize in space the military elite's synergistic dream by voluntarily disintegrating with his vehicle-weapon in a pyrotechnical apotheosis; for the ultimate metaphor of the speed-body is its final disappearance in the flames of explosion. *The possible rebirth of fascism is* a fear shown by many after the revelation of the Nazis' crimes against *humanity.* Whatever the case: since fascism never died, it doesn't need to be reborn. I'm not talking about little sadicomuseographic or commercial trifles, but quite simply the fact that it represented one of the most accomplished cultural, political and social revolutions of the dromocratic West, like the naval empires or the colonial establishments. And it certainly has less to fear from "the future" than does a Communism that no longer has anything Marxist about it but its name, and for which the end of the dictatorship of the proletariat was the admission of its historical failure.

Fascism is alive because total war, then total peace, have engaged the headquarters of the great national bodies (the armies, the forces of production) in a new spatial and temporal process, and the historical universe in a Kantian world. The problem is no longer one of a historiality in (chronological) time or (geographic) space, but in *what* space-time?

In a recent article, I stressed the necessity of reviewing our *physical concept of history*, of finally recognizing it for what it has become:

"…Which in short would make of war's conductibility (the coherent plan devised in time and space that can, through repetition, be imposed upon the enemy) not the instrument but the origin of a totalitarian language of History. This language is the mutual effort of the European States, then of the world, toward the absolute essence of foreign or civil war (speed), thus giving it the stature of an absolute takeover of world history by Western military intelligence. Pure history, then, is only the translation of a pure strategic advance over terrain. Its power is to precede and be final, and the historian is but a *captain in the war of time.*"[6]

4

The Consumption of Security

Security cannot be divided.

— Michel Poniatowski, March 4, 1976

"REVOLUTION GOES FASTER than the people," declared President-General Costa Gomes at the beginning of the Portugese events.

How could such a thing be possible? Simply because in the final account the West's so-called revolutions have never been made by the people, but by the military institution. Economic liberalism has been only a liberal pluralism of the order of speeds of penetration. To the heavy model of the hemmed in bourgeoisie, to the single schema of the weighty Marxist *mobil-machung* (ostensibly planned control of the movement of goods, persons, ideas), the West has long opposed the diversity of its logistical hierarchy, the utopia of a national wealth invested in automobiles, travel, movies, performances... A capitalism that has become one of jet-sets and instant-information banks, actually a whole *social illusion* subordinated to the strategy of the cold war. Let's make no mistake: whether it's the drop-outs, the beat generation, automobile drivers, migrant workers, tourists, olympic champions or travel agents, the military-industrial democracies have made every social category, without distinction, into *unknown soldiers of the order of speeds*—speeds whose hierarchy is controlled more and more each day by the State (headquarters), from the pedestrian to the rocket, from the metabolic to the technological.

In the 1960s, when a rich American wanted to prove his social success, he bought not "the biggest American car he could lay his hands on," but a "little European job," faster, less limited. To succeed is to reach the power of greater speed, to have the impression of escaping the unanimity of civic training. Since total war, there have been no foreign, external wars in the strict sense; as the Mayor of Philadelphia so aptly put it during a hot American summer: "Now the frontiers pass inside the cities." Whether highway or street, everything is part of the single glacis of the frontier desert.

The Berlin wall benefited in the summer of 1977 from the latest advances in mines and video systems—a veritable face-lift! After Belfast, Beirut showed us the old communal city crushed under the blows of the Palestinian migrants. What they lived through was not the old state of siege, but an aimless and permanent state of emergency. To survive in the city one had to stay informed daily, by radio, about the strategic situation of one's own neighborhood; everyone transformed his car into an assault vehicle, loaded with weapons in order to ensure freedom of movement. Not only didn't the violence distinguish between uniforms, but the combatants themselves veiled their faces, like members of a hold-up. They didn't want to be recognized even by their neighbors or social partners. They return to the state of the native combatant, to "open warfare"; a reappropriation of a certain technological under-development of the masses in the realm of weapons; a new progress of the disinformation of citizens, parallel to de-urbanization.

When the American State refuses to help New York in a time of crisis, when hospitals and schools have to shut down, when social aid is cut back and the city is no longer cleaned, it's the dissolution of the city in its own outskirts, the future popular self-government of civil fear. Popular war had largely contributed to making the means of survival on the battlefield into a means of existence. The modern State takes credit for the formula in its new logistical revolution: when the King of Morocco decides in the fall of 1975 to take back the Spanish Sahara, he sends not his armies, but "peace marchers," a miserable mass picked up in the cities and thrown unarmed into the desert at the front lines of the Moroccan tanks—as if, after all, it was now an ecological matter to be settled more between civilians than between military men.

With the Palestinian problem, popular war had suddenly taken on global proportions. Indeed, the tactic that consists in embracing in a diffuse manner the most widespread territories to escape the powerful nuclei of military repression could have no meaning for them, since the very cause of their struggle was the deprivation of geographic territory. They therefore lost no time in literally settling into the time zones of international airports. The new unknown combatants, come from nowhere and *no longer finding a strategic terrain, fight in strategic time, in the relativity of travel time.* Since in the final account there is no road that is not strategic, from this moment on there is no longer a truly civilian aviation. It is understandable that supersonics like the American SST, or more recently the Concorde, give rise to heated discussions: their high performances are a problem for the military. They reproduce in the vectors of the nuclear status quo the 1920s phenomenon of automotive assault in the streets of the bourgeois city.

On March 4, 1976, France's Michel Poniatowski, then-Minister of the Interior, declared, "Security cannot be divided!" But to be more precise, he should have said: From now on, security can no longer be divided. As then-President Giscard d'Estaing stated three months later in a speech at the Military Academy, "Alongside the supreme means of ensuring our security, we *need* the presence of security. In other words, we need *to have a social body organized around this need for security.*" On August 25, Olivier Stirn, Secretary of State in the Overseas Territories, told the Council of Ministers that "The evacuation of the inhabitants of Basse-Terre Island, who were threatened by the eruption of the Soufriere volcano, *demonstrated the possibilities for spontaneous action in a liberal society.*" As we saw later, civil and social protection in this type of affair is no longer contemporary with the catastrophe; it precedes and, if need be, invents it.[1]

In fact, the government's deliberately terroristic manipulation of the need for security is the perfect answer to all the new questions now being put to democracies by nuclear strategy—the new isolationism of the nuclear State that, in the U.S., for example, is totally revamping political strategy. They are trying to recreate *Union* through a new unanimity of need, just as the mass media phantasmatically created a need for cars, refrigerators... We will see the creation of a common feeling of insecurity that will lead to a new kind of consumption, the consumption of protection; this latter will progressively come to the fore and become *the target of the whole merchandising system.* This is essentially what Raymond Aron recently said, when he accused liberal society of having been too optimistic for too long! The indivisible promotion of the need for security already composes a new composite portrait of the citizen—no longer the one who enriches the nation by consuming, but the one who invests first and foremost in security, manages his own protection as best he can, and finally pays more to consume less.

All this is less contradictory than it seems. Capitalist society has always tightly linked politics with freedom from fear, social security with consumption and comfort. But as we saw, the other side of this obligatory movement is assistance; since the war of movement, the infirmity of unable bodies has taken on a social consistency through the demands of the military worker. If the Treaty of Versailles is concerned with assistance, it's because the inevitability of national Defense requires it, and henceforth imposes a plan of social action on the States as part of their general defense. As Gilbert Mury notes, the first true social workers were not *neutral* because they came from places like Colonel de la Roque's "French Social Party." It's a good thing to remember: the promoters of the new "Social Security" in Great Britain (Sir Beveridge, for example, in 1942) had made it an objective of total war. Furthermore, it was to encounter similar groups of fascist or Petainist inspiration on the European continent, such as the National Aid movement. It is interesting to note the enrollment in these movements of certain members of the fascist denunciation forces (who were formerly occupied with civilian surveillance and repression), their integration into the new personnel of social aid, as we take advantage of the experience of common-law prisoners today. This is because the activities of these technicians of standardization are inseparable from the hegemonic aims of the State administration.

The tasks of the "social worker" increase and change with the opportunities afforded. Currently known as a tutor, educator or group leader, he also performs other functions: after decolonization, the department of "native affairs" becomes the department of "social affairs"; in their own country the Portugese colonial troops establish a "ministry of social communication." And General Pinochet, who doesn't mince words, very simply creates in Chile a department of "civilian affairs!"

Several years ago in France, in a period of full economic prosperity, the social workers declared, "We are workers like any other because we repair the socio-productive apparatus." After '68, they were less sanguine: "The social workers feel very strongly the ambiguity of the notion of social work and are sensitive to the misunderstandings it can generate." In fact, in the new economy of survival, it is no longer a matter of participating in a society of (more or less futile) abundance. Mr. Berlinguer said it in January 1977: "*We* are the ones who want austerity, in order to change the system and construct a *new model of development.*" And strangely enough, he immediately refers to the transportation system, "to the revision of the myth of the personal automobile with the reorganization of cities. *The solution to the transportation problem should lead to a radical transformation of State mechanisms* through a modification of the nature of business." Thus, everywhere, the mobile mass's vehicular power is repressed and reduced; from limits on speed or fuel to the pure and simple suppression of the personal auto, the myth of the car is condemned to disappear along with the myth of the worker, the central historical agent of the logistical State.

The austerity preached by Enrico Berlinguer, as we know, had disastrous repercussions even within the Italian Communist Party, and many comparisons were made to the Spartan regime. But doubtless it would have been more correct to speak only of the end of the Lycurgean system, of the decomposition into anomie of a "society" whose members had been trained for centuries only to launch an attack, and who no longer knew what to do with their existence when this occupation was suddenly denied them. If you take away the Westerner's car or motorcycle, what will be left for him to do?—if not completely fulfill the prophecy of M.I.S. Bloch, who, in 1897, announced: "War having become a kind of stalemate in which neither side can gain the upper hand, the armies will remain face to face, constantly threatening each other but unable to strike the deciding blow. This is the future: no combat, only famine; no killing, only the bankruptcy of nations and the collapse of any social system."

In a social configuration whose precarious equilibrium is threatened by any ill-considered initiative, security can henceforth be likened to the absence of movement. The extended proletarianization of the suppression of wills can be likened to the suppression of gestures, for which the rise in unemployment is the best and most obvious image. We redistribute social work; we spotlight the performances of the physically and mentally handicapped, their records in olympics for the disabled; we impose the new belief that a body's inability to move is not really a serious problem. *Strangely* enough again, the army can be found behind these *philanthropic* enterprises. Read the memoirs of Abbot Oziol, the French country priest who created centers for retarded children from nothing, centers designed to tear them away from the psychiatric wards: "A visitor may sometimes be surprised to hear us say that one of our children is 'in the army.' That doesn't mean that our unfortunate little retard was called into the service. We simply mean by this to designate the building that was given us by the Military Treasury, which since then has given us so much other help." And it was General Malbec, director of the same National Military Treasury, who uttered the terrible slogan of these centers: "From the cradle to the grave!" But the army has never been anything else…

The redistribution of social aid finally aims at making the handicap functional, as the old Prussian State did in 1914. Financial aid takes on the appearance of a remuneration, a salary, at a time when the government insists on rewarding citizens who by denunciation act like auxilliary policemen. The indivisible security discerns in the bitter old man, excluded from the economic system by his modest pension and revenue, a last proletarian, a kind of attentive sentinel, immobile in the middle of the frenetic agitation of the social environment. One begins to meet these otherworldly beings in the street, aged persons whose wrists are equipped with an electronic alarm system scarcely larger than a wristwatch and relayed to a monitoring center. Gilbert Cotteau is at the origin of this kind of social action with the "Delta 7 Foundation," which is responsible for many things, but which also had recourse, in order to get off the ground, to financial aid from the armed forces (particularly the Air Force). Its beneficiaries were mainly Vietnamese children made deaf by the bombardments, who received hearing aids; or old persons who were given free telephones, complete with an alarm system hooked into the central police computer. Behind this operation we find the National Union of Social Aid Offices and the Ministry of Health, as well as the Ministry of the Interior.

The posters that launched the great campaign for the safety of senior citizens, the audio-visual spots: all this indoctrination is widely broadcast in old people's homes, clubs, hostels like so many orders for police mobilization, all of it furnished free for the asking.

For other social strata, manipulation of the need for security takes different forms. Since antiquity, precious metals, the gold standard, has been a "refuge value," a remedy for anxiety, and thus a symbol of individual security—this "insurance" value having been, as we know, freely transferred to a multitude of exchange systems. Nonetheless, the current questioning of the gold refuge as basic standard of the monetary system is quite reminiscent of the events of the Law Bank shortly before the French Revolution. It contributes to the collapse of social "security;" and we find here, in the midst of the nuclear status quo, the reasons that made the Spartan State refuse the use of precious metals as one of the consequences of non-war. (The State, careful to put the people's vigilance in defense to full use, deprived individuals of the means of protecting themselves other than by becoming totally engaged in the Lacedaemonian war machine.)

The code of production itself always aims at the "infinite receptacle of consumption." But the latter becomes the consumption of total security; the utopian use of defense reflexes leads us to modify esthetics and the nature of production. The meaning of business reform is totally different from the one ascribed to it by the powers that be. Thus, the appearance on the market of "nonbrand name products that are just as good"—which passed more or less unnoticed—seems to me to be a considerable event: merchandise in large demand is presented for reasons of "economy," in "anonymous" white labels, the company's obtrusive trade mark having disappeared. They are promoted with an immense anti-publicity campaign. They are, so we are told, "free products;" in other words they no longer rely on the dubious methods of whorish old marketing techniques. From now on, repulsion sells more than attraction; this is what organizes our new social existence around the objects of protection. If the companies are asked by the consumer protection agencies to moderate their advertising campaigns, it's because other forces of production seek to develop theirs in the area of information, like the members of the above-mentioned National Defense institute.

After the war of the domestic market, the war of the military market. It is no longer a system of consumption/production aiming at a democratic alliance, but the system of objects seeking to directly elect the military class or, more accurately, a technological and industrial development in the area of weaponry.

After his failed bid in the Portugese elections in April 1976, Mario Snares declared: "I don't need to govern with politicians; I can do it just as well with soldiers and specialists." The new Chinese leaders spout the same discourse. "Military socialism" wasn't born in Peru or Portugal in 1976, any more than it first appeared in Berlin in the 1930s or in the last century with Bismarck, Napoleon III and "social imperialism." The elimination of the political bourgeoisie's partner is only the realization of a strategic dream based solely on scientific and technological speculation: militarized nations that can do without armies (General Gallois' minimum vital force).

For Clausewitz, the political State is already a *"non-conducting medium*, a barrier that prevents *full discharge."* In such a statement, the nature of the military class's ambition is perfectly revealed and the atomic situation projected… "Under Bonaparte (general/chief of State), war was waged *without respite* until the enemy succumbed, and the counter-blows were struck with almost equal energy. Surely it is both natural and inescapable that this phenomenon should cause us to turn again to *the pure concept of war* with all its rigorous implications." Dynamic efficiency is the State machine's primary quality, and the nuclear State, ultimate stage of dromological progress, ensures the concept's cohesion thanks to the strategic calculator. Faced with and boarded by this ultimate war machine stands the last military proletarian, the henceforth will-less body of the President of the Republic, supreme commander of a vanished army. The President's body resembles those of the ancient conscripts caught between two fires. His final act will once again be Assault.

Part 4

THE STATE OF EMERGENCY

The State of Emergency

Speed is the essence of war.

— Sun Tzu

THE REDUCTION OF distances has become a strategic reality bearing incalculable economic and political consequences, since it corresponds to the negation of space.

The maneuver that once consisted in *giving up ground to gain Time* loses its meaning: at present, gaining Time is exclusively a matter of vectors. Territory has lost its significance in favor of the projectile. *In fact, the strategic value of the non-place of speed has definitively supplanted that of place*, and the question of possession of Time has revived that of territorial appropriation.

In this geographic contraction, which resembles the terrestrial movement described by Alfred Wegener, the binomial "fire movement" takes on a new meaning: the distinction between fire's *power to destroy* and the *power to penetrate* of movement, of the vehicle, is losing its "validity."[1]

With the supersonic vector (airplane, rocket, airwaves), penetration and destruction become one. The instantaneousness of action at a distance corresponds to the defeat of the unprepared adversary, but also, and especially, to the defeat of the world as a field, as distance, as matter.

Immediate penetration, or penetration that is approaching immediacy, becomes identified with the instantaneous destruction of environmental conditions, since after *space-distance*, we now lack *time-distance* in the increasing acceleration of vehicular performances (precision, distance, speed).

From this point on, the binomial *fire-movement* exists only to designate a double movement of implosion and explosion; *the power of implosion* revives the old subsonic vehicles' (means of transportation, projectiles) power to penetrate, and *the power of explosion* revives the destructive power of classical molecular explosives. In this paradoxical object, *simultaneously explosive and implosive*, the new war machine combines a double disappearance: *the disappearance of matter in nuclear disintegration* and *the disappearance of places in vehicular extermination.*

Nonetheless, we should note that the disintegration of matter is constantly deferred in the deterrent equilibrium of peaceful coexistence, but not so the extermination of distances. In less than half a century, geographical spaces have kept shrinking as speed has increased. And if at the beginning of the 1940s we still had to count the speed of naval "strike power"—the major destructive power of the time—*in knots*, by the beginning of the 1960s this rapidity was measured *in machs*, in other words in thousands of kilometers per hour. And it is likely that current high energy research will soon allow us to reach the speed of light with laser weapons.

If, as Lenin claimed, "strategy means choosing which points we apply force to," we must admit that these "points," today, are no longer *geostrategic strongpoints*, since from *any given spot* we can now reach any other, no matter where it may be, in record time and within several meters...

We have to recognize that *geographic localization* seems to have definitively lost its strategic value and, inversely, that this same value is attributed *to the delocalization of the vector*, of a vector in permanent movement—no matter if this movement is aerial, spatial, underwater or underground. All that counts is the speed of the moving body and the undetectability of its path.

From the war of movement of mechanized forces, we reach the *strategy of Brownian movements*, a kind of chronological and pendular war that revives ancient popular and geographic warfare by a geostrategic homogenization of the globe. This homogenization was already announced in the nineteenth century, notably by the Englishman Mackinder in his theory of the "World-Island," in which Europe, Asia and Africa would compose a single continent to the detriment of the Americas—a theory that seems to have come to fruition today with the disqualification of localizations. But we should note that the indifferentiation of geostrategic positions is not the only effect of vectorial performances, for after the homogenization sought and finally acquired by naval and aerial imperialism, *strategic spatial miniaturization* is now the order of the day.

In 1955 General Chassin stated, "The fact that the earth is round has not been sufficiently studied from the military point of view." No sooner said than done. But in the ballistic progress of weapons, the curvature of the earth has not stopped shrinking. It is no longer the continents that become agglomerated, but the totality of the planet that is diminished, depending on the progress of the arms "race." The continental translation that, curiously enough, we find both in the geophysician Wegener, with the drift of land masses, and in Mackinder, with the geopolitical amalgam of lands, has given way to a world wide phenomenon of terrestrial and technological contraction that today makes us penetrate into an artificial topological universe: *the direct encounter of every surface on the globe.*

The ancient inter-city duel, war between nations, the permanent conflict between naval empires and continental powers have all suddenly disappeared, giving way to an unheard of opposition: *the juxtaposition of every locality, all matter.* The planetary mass becomes no more than a "critical mass," a precipitate resulting from the extreme reduction of contact time, a fearsome friction of places and elements that only yesterday were still distinct and separated by a buffer of distances, which have suddenly become anachronistic. In *The Origin of Continents and Oceans,* published in 1915, Alfred Wegener writes that in the beginning *the earth can only have had but one face,* which seems likely, given the capacities for interconnection. In the future the earth will have but one interface...

If speed thus appears as the essential fall out of styles of conflicts and cataclysms, the current "arms race" is in fact only "*the arming of the race" toward the end of the world as distance, in other words as a field of action.*

The term "deterrence" points to the ambiguity of this situation, in which the weapon replaces the protection of armor, in which the possibilities of offense and offensive ensure in and of themselves the defense, the entire defensive against the "explosive" dimension of strategic arms, but not at all against the "implosive" dimension of the vectors' performances, since on the contrary the maintenance of a credible "strike power" requires the constant refining of the engines' power, in other words of their ability to reduce geographic space to nothing or almost nothing.

In fact, without the violence of speed, that of weapons would not be so fearsome. *In the current context, to disarm would thus mean first and foremost to decelerate*, to defuse the race toward the end. *Any treaty that does not limit the speed of this race* (the speed of means of communicating destruction) *will not limit strategic arms*, since from now on the essential object of strategy consists in maintaining the non-place of a general delocalization of means that alone still allows us to gain fractions of seconds, which gain is indispensable to any freedom of action. As General Fuller wrote, "When the combatants threw javelins at each other, the weapon's initial speed was such that one could see it on its trajectory and parry its effects with one's shield. But when the javelin was replaced by the bullet, the speed was so great that parry became impossible." Impossible to move one's body out of the way, but possible if one moved out of the weapon's range; possible as well through the shelter of the trench, greater than that of the shield—possible, in other words, through space and matter.

Today, the reduction of warning time that results from the supersonic speeds of assault leaves so little time for detection, identification and response that in the case of a surprise attack the supreme authority would have to risk abandoning his supremacy of decision by authorizing the lowest echelon of the defense system to immediately launch anti-missile missiles. The two political superpowers have thus far preferred to avoid this situation through negotiations, renouncing anti-missile defense at the same time.

Given the lack of space, an active defense requires at least the material time to intervene. But *these* are the "war materials" that disappear in the acceleration of the means of communicating destruction. There remains only a passive defense that consists less in reinforcing itself against the megaton powers of nuclear weapons than in a series of constant, unpredictable, aberrant movements, movements which are thus strategically effective—for at least a little while longer, we hope. In fact, war now rests entirely on the deregulation of time and space. This is why the *technical* maneuver that consists in complexifying the vector by constantly improving its performances has now totally supplanted *tactical* maneuvers on the terrain, as we have seen. General Ailleret points this out in his history of weapons by stating that *the definition of arms programs has become one of the essential elements of strategy.* If in ancient conventional warfare we could still talk about army maneuvers in the fields, in the current state of affairs, if this maneuver still exists, it no longer needs a "field." The invasion of the instant succeeds the invasion of the territory. The countdown becomes the scene of battle, the final frontier.

The opposing sides can easily ban bacteriological, geodesic or meteorological warfare. In reality, what is currently at stake with strategic arms limitation agreements (SALT I) is no longer the explosive but the vector, *the vector of nuclear deliverance*, or more precisely its performances. The reason for this is simple: where the molecular or nuclear explosive's blast made a given area unfit for existence, that of the implosive (vehicles and vectors) suddenly reduces reaction time, and the time for political decision, to nothing. If over thirty years ago the nuclear explosive completed the cycle of *spatial wars*, at the end of this century the implosive (beyond politically and economically invaded territories) inaugurates *the war of time*. In full peaceful coexistence, without any declaration of hostilities, and more surely than by any other kind of conflict, rapidity delivers us from this world. We have to face the facts: today, speed is war, the last war.

But let's go back to 1962, to the crucial events of the Cuban missile crisis. At that time, the two superpowers had *fifteen minutes*' warning time for war. The installation of Russian rockets on Castro's island threatened to reduce the Americans' warning to thirty seconds, which was unacceptable for President Kennedy, whatever the risks of his categorical refusal. We all know what happened: the installation of a *direct line*—the "hot line"—and the interconnection of the two Heads of State!

Ten years later, in 1972, when the normal warning time was down to several minutes—ten for ballistic missiles, a mere two for satellite weapons—Nixon and Brezhnev signed the first strategic arms limitation agreement in Moscow. In fact, this agreement aims less at the quantitative limitation of weapons (as its adversary/partners claim) than at the preservation of a properly "human" political power, since the constant progress of rapidity threatens from one day to the next to reduce the warning time for nuclear war *to less than one fatal minute*—thus finally abolishing the Head of State's power of reflection and decision in favor of a pure and simple *automation* of defense systems. The decision for hostilities would then belong only to several strategic computer programs. *After having been* (because of its destructive capacities) *the equivalent of total war*—the nuclear missile launching submarine alone is able to destroy 500 cities—*the war machine suddenly becomes* (thanks to the reflexes of the strategic calculator) *the very decision for war*.

What will remain, then, of the "political reasons" for deterrence? Let us recall that in 1962, among the reasons that made General de Gaulle decide to have the populations ratify the decision to elect the President of the Republic by universal suffrage, there was the credibility of deterrence, the legitimacy of the referendum being a fundamental element of this very deterrence. What will remain of all this in the automation of deterrence? in the automation of decision?

The transition *from the state of siege* of wars of space to *the state of emergency* of the war of time only took several decades, during which the political era of the statesman was replaced by the apolitical era of the State apparatus. Facing the advent of such a regime, we would do well to wonder about what is much more than a temporal phenomenon.

At the close of our century, *the time of the finite world is coming to an end*; we live in the beginnings of a paradoxical *miniaturization of action*, which others prefer to baptize *automation*. Andrew Stratton writes, "We commonly believe that automation suppresses the possibility of human error. In fact, it transfers that possibility from the action stage to the conception stage. We are now reaching the point where the possibilities of an accident during the critical minutes of a plane landing, if guided automatically, are fewer than if a pilot is controlling it. We might wonder if we will ever reach the stage of automatically controlled nuclear weapons, in which the margin of error would be less than with human decision. But the possibility of this progress threatens to reduce to little or nothing the time for human decision to intervene in the system."

This is brilliant. Contraction in time, the disappearance of the territorial space, after that of the fortified city and armor, leads to a situation in which the notions of "before" and "after" designate only the future and the past in a form of war that causes the "present" to disappear in the instantaneousness of decision.

The final power would thus be less one of imagination than of anticipation, so much so that to govern would be *no more than* to foresee, simulate, memorize the simulations; that the present "Research Institute" could appear to be the blueprint of this final power, the power of utopia.

The loss of material space leads to the government of nothing but time. *The Ministry of Time* sketched in each vector will finally be accomplished following the dimensions of the biggest vehicle there is, the *State-vector.* The whole geographic history of the distribution of land and countries would stop in favor of a single *regrouping of time*, power no longer being comparable to anything but a "meteorology." In this precarious fiction speed would suddenly become a destiny, a form of progress, in other words a "civilization" in which each speed would be something of a "region" of time.

As Mackinder said, forces of pressure are always exerted in the same direction. Now, this single direction of geopolitics is that which leads to the immediate *commutation* of things and places. War is not, as Foch claimed, harboring illusions on the future of chemical explosives, "a worksite of fire." War has always been a worksite of movement, a speed-factory. *The technological breakthrough,* the last form of the war of movement, ends up, with deterrence, at the dissolution of what *separated* but also *distinguished*, and this non-distinction corresponds for us to a political blindness.

We can verify it with General de Gaulle's decree of January 7, 1959, suppressing the distinction between peacetime and wartime. Furthermore, during this same period, and despite the Vietnamese exception that proves the rule, war has shrunk from several years to several days, even to several hours.

In the 1960s a mutation occurs: *the passage from wartime to the war of peacetime*, to that *total peace* that others still call "peaceful coexistence." The blindness of the speed of means of communicating destruction is not a liberation from geopolitical servitude, but the extermination of space as the field of freedom of political action. We only need refer to the necessary controls and constraints of the railway, airway or highway infrastructures to see the fatal impulse: the more speed increases, the faster freedom decreases.

The apparatus' self-propulsion finally entails the self-sufficiency of automation. What happens in the example of the racecar driver, who is no more than a worried lookout for the catastrophic probabilities of his movement, is reproduced on the political level as soon as conditions require an action in real time.[2]

Let us take, for example, a crisis situation: "From the very beginning of the Six Days' War in 1967, President Johnson took control of the White House, one hand guiding the Sixth Fleet, the other on the hot line. The necessity of the link between the two became clearly apparent as soon as an Israeli attack against the American reconnaissance ship *Liberty* provoked the intervention of one of the fleet's aircraft carriers. Moscow examined every blip on the radar screens as attentively as Washington did: would the Russians interpret the air planes' change of course and their convergence as an act of aggression? This is where the hot line came in: Washington immediately explained the reasons for this operation and Moscow was reassured" (Harvey Wheeler).

In this example of strategic political action in real time, the Chief of State is in fact a "Great Helmsman." But the prestigious nature of the people's historical guide gives way to the more prosaic and rather banal one of a "test pilot" trying to maneuver his machine in a very narrow margin. Ten years have passed since this "crisis state," and the arms race has caused the margin of political security to narrow still further, bringing us closer to the critical threshold where the possibilities for properly human political action will disappear in a "State of Emergency;" where telephone communication between statesmen will stop, probably in favor of an interconnection of computer systems, modern calculators of strategy and, consequently, of politics. (Let us recall that the computers' first task was to solve simultaneously a series of complex equations aimed at causing the trajectory of the anti-aircraft projectile and that of the airplane to meet.)

Here we have the fearsome telescoping of elements born of the "amphibious generations"; the extreme proximity of parties *in which the immediacy of information immediately creates the crisis;* the frailty of reasoning power, which is but the effect of a miniaturization of action—the latter resulting from the miniaturization of space as a field of action.

An imperceptible movement on a computer keyboard, or one made by a "skyjacker" brandishing a cookie box covered with masking tape, can lead to a catastrophic chain of events that until recently was inconceivable. We are too willing to ignore the fact that, alongside the threat of proliferation resulting from the acquisition of nuclear explosives by irresponsible parties, there is a proliferation of the threat resulting from the vectors that cause those who own or borrow them to become just as irresponsible.

In the beginning of the 1940s, Paris was a six-days' walk from the border, a three-hours' drive, and one hour by plane. Today the capital is only several minutes away from anywhere else, and anywhere else is only several minutes away from its end—so much so that the tendency, which still existed several years ago, *to advance* one's destructive means closer to the enemy territory (as in the Cuban missile crisis) is reversing. The present tendency is toward geographic disengagement, a movement of *retreat* that is due only to the progress of the vectors and to the extension of their reach (cf. the American submarine *Trident*, whose new missiles can travel 8 to 10,000 kilometers, as opposed to the *Poseidon's* 4 to 5,000).

Thus, the different strategic nuclear forces (American and Soviet) will no longer need to patrol the area in the target continents; they can henceforth retreat within their territorial limits. This is confirmation that they are abandoning a form of geostrategic conflict. After the reciprocal renunciation of geodesic war, we will possibly see the abandonment of advanced bases, extending to America's extraordinary abandonment of its sovereignty over the Panama Canal… A sign of the times, of the time of the war of time.

Nonetheless, we must note that this strategic retreat no longer has anything in common with *the retreat* that allowed conventional armies to "gain time by losing ground." In the retreat due to the extended reach of the ballistic vectors, *we in fact gain time by losing the space of the (stationary or mobile) advanced bases, but this time is gained at the expense of our own forces,* of the performances of our own engines, and not at the enemy's expense, since, symmetrically, the latter accompanies this geostrategic disengagement. *Everything suddenly happens as if each protagonist's own arsenal became his (internal) enemy, by advancing too quickly.* Like the recoil of a firearm, the implosive movement of the ballistic performances diminishes the field of strategic forces. In fact, if the adversary/partners didn't pull back their means of communicating destruction while lengthening their reach, the higher speed of these means would already have reduced the time of decision about their use to nothing. Just as in 1972, in Moscow, the partners in this game abandoned plans for an anti-missile missile defense, so five years later they wasted the advantage of swiftness for the very temporary benefit of a greater extension of their intercontinental missiles. Both seem to fear—all the while seeking—the multiplying effect of speed, of that *speed activity* so dear to all armies since the Revolution.

In the face of this curious contemporary *regression* of stragetic arms limitation agreements, it is wise to return to the very principle of deterrence. The essential aim of throwing ancient weapons or of shooting off new ones has never been to kill the enemy or destroy his means, but to deter him, in other words, to *force him to interrupt his movement.* Regardless of whether this physical movement is one that allows the assailed to contain the assailant or one of invasion, "the aptitude for war is the aptitude for movement," which a Chinese strategist expressed in these words: "An army is always strong enough when it can come and go, spread out and regroup, as it wishes and when it wishes."

For the last several years, however, this freedom of movement has been hindered not by the enemy's capacity for resistance or reaction, but by the refinement of the vectors used. Deterrence seems to have passed suddenly from the fire stage, in other words the explosive stage, to that of the movement of vectors, as if a final degree of nuclear deterrence had appeared, still poorly mastered by the actors in the global strategic game. Here again, we must return to the strategic and tactical realities of weaponry in order to grasp the present logistical reality. As Sun Tzu said, "Weapons are tools of ill omen." They are first feared and fearsome as *threats*, long before being used. Their "ominous" character can be split into three components:

The threat of their performance at the moment of their invention, of their production;

The threat of their use against the enemy;

The effect of their use, which is fatal for persons and destructive for their goods.

If these last two components are unfortunately known, and have long been experimented with, the firsι, on the other hand, *the (logistical) ill omen of the invention of their performance,* is less commonly recognized. Nonetheless, it is at this level that the question of deterrence is raised. *Can we deter an enemy from inventing new weapons, or from perfecting their performances?* Absolutely not.

We thus find ourselves facing this dilemma:

The threat of use (the second component) of the nuclear arm prohibits the terror of actual use (the third component). But for this threat to remain and allow the strategy of deterrence, we are forced to develop the threatening system that characterizes the first component: the *ill omen of the appearance of new performances for the means of communicating destruction*. Stated plainly, this is the perpetual sophistication of combat means and the replacement of the geostrategic breakthrough by the technological breakthrough, the great logistical maneuvers.

We must face the facts: if ancient weapons deterred us from interrupting movement, *the new weapons deter us from interrupting the arms race*. Moreover, they require in their technological (dromological) logic the exponential development, not of *the number* of destructive machines, since their power has increased (simply compare the millions of projectiles in the two World Wars to the several thousands of rockets in contemporary arsenals), but of their global *performances.* Destructive capabilities having reached the very limits of possibility with thermonuclear arms, the enemy's "logistical strategies" are once more oriented toward power of penetration and flexibility of use.

The balance of terror is thus a mere illusion in the industrial stage of war, in which reigns a perpetual imbalance, a constantly raised bid, able to invent new means of destruction without end. We have proven ourselves, on the other hand, not only quite incapable of destroying those we've already produced (the "waste products" of the military industry being as hard to recycle as those of the nuclear industry), but especially incapable of avoiding the threat of their appearance.

War has thus moved from the action stage to the conception stage that, as we know, characterizes *automation.* Unable to control the emergence of new means of destruction, deterrence, for us, is tantamount to setting in place a series of automatisms, reactionary industrial and scientific procedures from which all political choice is absent. By becoming "strategic," in other words, by combining offense and defense, the new weapons deter us from interrupting the movement of the arms race, and the "logistical strategy" of their production becomes the inevitable production of destructive means as an obligatory factor of non-war—a vicious circle in which the inevitability of production replaces that of destruction. The war machine is now not only all of war, *but also becomes the adversary/partners' principal enemy* by depriving them of their freedom of movement.[3] Dragged unwillingly into the "servitude without honor" of deterrence, the protagonists henceforth practice the "politics of the worst," or more precisely, the "apolitics of the worst," which necessarily leads to the war machine one day becoming the very decision for war—thus accomplishing the perfection of its self-sufficiency, *the automation of deterrence.*

The suggestive juxtaposition of the terms *deterrence* and *automation* allows us to understand better the structural axis of contemporary military-political events, as H. Wheeler specifies: "Technologically possible, centralization has become politically necessary." This shortcut recalls that of Saint-Just's famous dictum: "When a people can be oppressed, it will be"—the difference being that this techno-logistical oppression no longer concerns only the "people," but the "deciders" as well. If only yesterday the freedom of maneuver (that aptitude for movement which has been equated with the aptitude for war) occasionally required delegations of power up to the secondary echelons, the reduction of the margin of maneuver due to the progress of the means of communicating destruction causes an extreme concentration of responsibilities for the solitary decision-maker that the Chief of State has become. This contraction is, however, far from being complete; it continues according to the arms race, at the speed of the new capacities of the vectors, until one day it will dispossess this last man. In fact, the movement is the same that restrains the number of projectiles and that reduces to nothing or almost nothing the decision of an individual deprived of counsel. The maneuver is the same as the one that today leads us to abandon territories and advanced bases, and as the one that will one day lead us to renounce solitary human decision in favor of the absolute miniaturization of the political field which is *automation.*

If in Frederick the Great's time *to win was to advance,* for the supporters of deterrence it is *to retreat,* to leave places, peoples and the individual where they are—to the point where dromological progress closely resembles the jet engine's reaction propulsion, caused by the ejection of a certain quantity of movement (the product of a mass times a velocity) *in the direction opposite to the one we wish to take.*

In this *war of recession* between East and West—contemporary not with the illusory limitation of strategic arms, but with *the limitation of strategy itself*—the power of thermonuclear explosion serves as an artificial horizon for a race that is increasing the power of the vehicular implosion. The impossibility of interrupting the progress of the power of penetration, other than by an *act of faith* in the enemy, leads us to deny strategy as *prior knowledge.* The automatic nature not only of arms and means, but also of the command, is the same as denying our ability to reason: *Nicht raisonniren!* Frederick the Second's order is perfected by a deterrence that leads us to reduce our freedom not only of action and decision, but also of conception. The logic of arms systems is eluding the military framework more and more, and moving toward the engineer responsible for research and development—in expectation, of course, of the system's self sufficiency. Two years ago Alexandre Sanguinetti wrote, "It is becoming less and less conceivable to build attack planes, which with their spare parts cost several million dollars each, to transport bombs able to destroy a country railroad station. *It is simply not cost-effective.*" This logic of practical war, in which the operating costs of the (aerial) vector automatically entail the heightening of its destructive capability because of the requirements of transporting a tactical nuclear weapon, is not limited to attack planes; it is also becoming the logic of the State apparatus. This backwardness is the logistical consequence of producing means to communicate destruction. *The danger of the nuclear weapon, and of the arms system it implies, is thus not so much that it will explode, but that it exists and is imploding in our minds.*

Let us summarize this phenomenon:

— Two bombs interrupt the war in the Pacific, and several dozen nuclear submarines are enough to ensure peaceful coexistence...

This is its *numerical* aspect.

— With the appearance of the multiple thermonuclear warhead and the rapid development of tactical nuclear arms, we see the miniaturization of explosive charges...

This is its *volumetric* aspect.

— After having cleared the planet surface of a cumbersome defensive apparatus by reducing undersea and underground strategic arms, they renounce world expanse by reducing the trouble spots and advanced bases...

This is its *geographical* aspect.

— Once responsible for the operations, the old chiefs of war, strategists and generals, find themselves demoted and restricted to simple maintenance operations, for the sole benefit of the Chief of State...

This is its *political* aspect.

But this quantitative and qualitative scarcity doesn't stop. Time itself is no longer enough:

— Constantly heightened, the vectors' already quasi-supersonic capacities are superseded by the high enegies that enable us to approach the speed of light...

This is its *spatio-temporal* aspect.

After the time of the State's political relativity as nonconducting medium, we are faced with the no time of the politics of relativity. The *full discharge* feared by Clausewitz has come about with the State of Emergency. The violence of speed has become both the location and the law, the world's destiny and its destination.

— September 1977

Notes

Part I. The Dromocratic Revolution

1. From Street Fight to State Right

1. The Parisian press popularized the term following an attack on a city vehicle by a band of hoodlums whose mastermind was the famous "Golden Helmet."

2. *Kampf um Berlin*, published two years before the national socialists took power in 1931, and dedicated by Joseph Goebbels "to the Party's old guard in Berlin."

3. Dromomaniacs. Name given to deserters under the *ancien régime*, and in psychiatry to compulsive walkers.

4. Marinetti, with commentary by Giovanni Lista. "*Poètes d'Aujourd'hui*" series, Paris.

5. "Circulation Habitable," *Architecture Principe*, no. 3, April 1966.

6. Cf. Lewis Mumford, *The City in History* (New York, 1961), et al.

7. *Ibid.* The presence of land was considered sufficient in and of itself before the advent of speculation.

8. Paul Virilio, *L'insécurité du Territoire* (Paris, 1976); p. 77ff.

9. Course in permanent fortification at the School for the Application of Engineering and Artillery, 1888. Quoted by Vauban.

10, *Ibid.*

11. *Ibid.* Here again the military remarks rejoin the schema of the urban fortress. From the outset, the city is where the problems of health and evacuation of "waste" are posed. Already in the fourteenth century, the problem of pollution preoccupied the British parliament.

12. Vauban by Colonel Lazard, 1934. In Weygand's preface we read: "The author picks up in Vauban's writings the expression 'fortified country,' which he judiciously likens to 'fortified regions.' Isn't the man of genius always something of a precursor? When Colonel Lazard studies more specifically the engineer in the great man of war, he tries to clear him of the accusation of formalism. *He states and proves that the true system of Vauban consisted in applying the fortification to the terrain.* We have found no better system in these last years when it came to protecting our own soil."

13. The Parisian Hanse, those who would have been called "water merchants who deal on the use of rivers." (Volume XVIII of the Old French Laws).

2. From Highway Right to State Right

1. While at the same time, the arms industries are already employing production groups of 5,000 workers.

2. *La France et les huit heures* by Andre-François Poncet and Emile Mireaux, 1922.

3. The confession is superceded. In the Middle Ages, the question is put to a body under torture, one that "knows the truth" and must let it escape in spite of himself. In the nineteenth century, torture is abolished not out of humanitarianism, but because they realized that any act (every human movement) leaves external traces, an involuntary stamp. From then on, *they scientifically make proofs talk,* they make them, in a sense, "confess" in place of the suspect by arranging these material traces in a coherent discourse/path. Because their justice was handed down from very early on in the theatrical form of a dialogue, the Anglo-Saxons rapidly verified that from identical sets of material proofs they could draw different coherent discourses, each cancelling the other out, by simply changing the order of the elements. Psychoanalysis in some sense took up where this left off by substituting for the materialness of external traces the internal marks of crime. The psychiatric confession is obtained from the subject in spite of himself; it crosses his lips by force, but in the form of incoherent traces and materials that will be reconstituted according to the schemas of psychoanalytic science. Not only is the persistent flow of the psychoanalytic confession *not* dependent on the subject's will, but it doesn't even concern the instant of his crime, the circumstances that only the subject knows. Rather, it concerns a totality going from the accused's birth to the diagnostic of a final judgment. If in these tests someone is still listening for a confession, it is evident that this confession is no longer the story of a crime by its author. This was completed notably by the mapping of heavy crime zones in urban planning systems, and beyond this by the "criminostat" (computer aided visualization of statistical fields) currently being tested by the police. We could imagine that at this level the gaps and hazards inherent in

the ordering of materials should disappear, since with computers they could make the accusing discourse perfectly coherent, or at least approaching perfect coherence, having to do both with the name of the subject and that of the object. At that point, they could do totally without the confession of the accused, who would be less informed about his own crime than the computer, and who, no longer being the one who knows "the truth," would have nothing left to confess,

Part II. The Dromocratic Progress

1. From Space Right to State Right

1. F. Thiede and E. Schmahe, *Die Fliegende Nation*, Berlin, 1933.

2. "Since the end of the seventeenth century, the *fleet in being*, a name thought up by Admiral Herbert, had marked the passage from *being* to *becoming* in the exercise of constraint on the adversary. It meant the end of the naval apparatus and of war waged at short distances; the number and firepower of the vessels in the front lines became secondary." Paul Virilio, *L'insecurité du territoire*, Paris, 1976.

3. Administrative correspondence under Louis XIV.

4. "Materialism is the true son of Great Britain." Marx, *Contribution to the History of French Materialism.*

5. Cf. Marinetti, *Futurist Manifesto*, *Tactile Navigation*, and Giovanni Lista's commentary, *Marinetti.*

6. Peace of war, peace of exhaustion (Briand): "No one today can still wish to see the international regime of 1939 revived, for in fact, at that time, it was already no more than the ruins of a system." Papers of the Society of Nations on the passage from war economy to peacetime economy, May 1943.

7. The confession is superseded; all the information gathered by the police territorial brigades end up in the central computer of the National Police headquarters in Rosny-sous-Bois: *criminostat* (visualization of statistical fields).

2. Practical War

1. The Engineering Corps' technological reply to the totalitarian empires of naval engineering and liberal capitalism.

2. Abel Ferry, *La guerre vue d'en bas et d'en haut* (letters, notes, speeches and reports), Paris, 1920. The Vosges deputy, killed in the service of France on September

15, 1918, left his wife the task of publishing his work "immediately following the total demobilization of the French army and without taking into account the demands of interested parties ...," "a double lesson from the battlefield and from the Council of Ministers, preaching, from the very first months of war, the necessity for parliamentary control," Many passages commented on here have been taken from this capital work.

Part III. The Dromocratic Society

1. Unable Bodies

1. Pierre Nord, *Double crime sur la Ligne Maginot.*

2. August 1977: the American Congress allows the World Bank to extend credit to Vietnam, but also to Cambodia and Angola.

3. Sparta armed itself in view of accomplishing its *tour de force*: "We could scarcely help but see in this adaptation something other than an automatic evolution. The methodical and tenacious fashion in which everything was oriented toward a single goal obliges us to recognize the intervention of a conscious organizer. It is necessary to posit *the existence of one or two men*, working in concert, who transformed primitive institutions to make them the *agoge* and the Cosmos." M.P. Nilsson, "Die grundlagen des spartanischen Lebens"; in *Klio*, volume XII.

4. "Sparta paid the penalty for having taken her own headstrong course at the parting of the ways in the eighth century B.C. by condemning herself in the sixth century to standing still—with arms presented like a solider on parade—at a moment when the other Hellenes were just moving forward once again on one of the most signal moves in the whole course of Hellenic history." Arnold .J. Toynbee, *War and Civilization*, Oxford University Press, 1955.

5. Georges Huppert, *L'idée de l'histoire parfaite*, 1973.

6. Before history as poem or mythic chant, there is the mechanism of the trance and the persistence of those short invocations which create unanimity: "We are not warriors. But suddenly we believe we are, and the war begins" (Leiris). This is also the aim of the psychological training of elite corps, of political meetings, of military ceremonies... Inversely, the Spartan authorities discouraged their citizenry from cultivating music, "an art which," as Toynbee remarks, "is so near akin to the soldier's that, in our modern Western World, it is regarded as the best preparation for a military training." But the Spartans were also prohibited from competing in the great pan-Hellenic athletic sports. In a word, every allusion to kinetic progress was eliminated from the constitution.

7. Georges Duby, *The Early Growth of the European Economy: Warriors and Peasants*, Ithaca, 1974.

2. The Boarding of Metabolic Vehicles

1. *Trans.*: Untranslatable pun between *arraisonnement*, "the boarding of a ship for inspection," and *raisonnement*, "reasoning." Virilio will play on this throughout the chapter.

2. "Man is the passenger of woman, not only at birth but also in their sexual relations... Paraphrasing Samuel Butler, we could say that the female is the means the male has found to reproduce himself, in other words to *come into the world.* In this sense, woman is the species' first means of transport, its very first vehicle. The second would be the mounting and coupling of dissimilar bodies fitted out for migration, the voyage in common." Paul Virilio, *Métempsychose du passager*, May 1977.

3. *Trans.* A play on words: *bonne conduite* means both "good conduct" and "safe driving."

4. See notably the archives of Morimond (Haute-Marne region) and Clairvaux; the libraries of Besançon and Carpentras; *L'ordre de Calatrava* by Francis Gutton, 1955; etc.

5. Cf. Paul Virilio, *Negative Horizon.* London: Continuum, 2005.

6. Here we see perhaps one of the profound causes of Spartan opposition to any form of mobility as the preservation of the Lycurgean system.

3. The End of the Proletariat

1. *Trans.* A play on the word *meuble*, both "furniture" and "movable."

2. D. Crivelli, *La fin de la crise*, 1932. Proto-pop culture and European culture.

3. "Could I yet have imagined that this absolutely necessary historical evolution, in determined conditions, constituted a *retreat* of progress and *manufactured* men who were less than savages... Engels in the *Neue Rheinische Zeitung.*

4. Letter from Charles V to ambassador Ghislain de Busbecq.

5. "Human history is all an affair of chance." A statement that Heidegger, on the eve of total war, renders less freely than it would seem: "All greatness is in assault."

6. Cf. Paul Virilio, *Popular Defense and Ecological Struggles*, New York: Semiotext(e) Foreign Agents Series, 1986.

4. The Consumption of Security

1. The minister was to announce just as joyfully on November 20, 1976: "The Soufrière business is over!" According to the press, this "abortive eruption" had already cost—this was not a final figure—the sum of 200,000,000 francs by mid-October.

Part IV. The State of Emergency

1. Alfred Wegener, *The Origin of Continents and Oceans*, a theory of continental drift (fifth edition).

2. In terms of control, the meaning of this time is a function of the temporal field in which perception, decision and action are involved.

3. The missile-carrying nuclear submarine has in itself the destructive power of all the explosives used in the Second World War.

Other Semiotext(e) Titles by Paul Virilio

Speed & Politics

Popular Defense and Ecological Struggles

Aesthetics of Disappearance

Pure War with Sylvère Lotringer

Lost Dimension

Looking Back on the End of the World

Politics of the Very Worst

Crepuscular Dawn with Sylvère Lotringer

The Accident of Art with Sylvère Lotringer